What People Are Saying about "The Call"

"The Call is one of the most heartfelt, honest and truly inspiring accounts of the life journey of my teammate, who I am honored and humbled to also call my dear friend. Brian's story is a true testament of his devotion to the love of his life, Connie, and his beautiful family as well as his strong faith and unwavering determination to overcome any obstacle in life by always trusting in the Lord. No matter what your belief is or what challenges you may face, Brian's message will resonate with you."

-Bucky Dent
Starting shortstop for the New York Yankees in World Series Championships, 1977 and 1978

"Brian Doyle is my friend, teammate, and my hero. Read "The Call" and find out how this Christian gentleman has captured the love and respect of everyone he meets. Brian has faced many challenges in his life, but his faith in Christ has never wavered. I'm proud to call him my friend. The world needs more Brian Doyles."

-Ron Guidry
New York Yankees

"Brian's life story is important to read, he has proven to be a great athlete, instructor, mentor, spiritual leader and a loyal friend. Learning about his life will give spiritual inspiration and important life lessons to all."

-Chris Chambliss
Two-Time World Series Champ and
Golden Glove Recipient

"I have known Brian Doyle for over 30 years. His courage, integrity and faith have been an inspiration to me in my own walk with the Lord. This book will give you a look into Brian's journey, his battles, successes, and his heart."

-Bill Rose
Limited Partner New York Yankees

"I first met Brian Doyle on a Global Baseball Mission trip to Cuba. I was amazed at the man's ability to take a boys' game and use it to share the good news of our Lord and Savior. Brian's ability to love on people with a different language and different culture is phenomenal! If you are a baseball fan you will love this book. If you are not a fan, you will love this underdog story of a boy who was told he couldn't *make it*, prove his doubters wrong. You will love Brian Doyle, I know I do.

"Brian has a desire to finish strong, something men seem to have trouble doing today. I know this, Brian will do it, and he will give all Glory to our great and mighty God!"

-Ted Barrett
Major League Umpire, Crew Chief #65

"Brian Doyle was, is, and will always be an inspiration in my life. His exemplary attitude through all his misfortune is a lesson for us all. Words like 'do not be afraid', 'fear not', etc occur over three hundred times in the Bible and arguably 365 times, one for every day of the year. Brian is an example of strong faith and obeyed those words, "Fear Not!" A pitching coach once went to the mound and told the pitcher who was in a jam, "Throw strikes, Babe Ruth's dead." That's Brian. No fear."

-Ed Randall
Host, "Ed Randall's Talking Baseball" on WFAN-Radio in New York and "Remember When" on Sirius/XM Radio, (Brian's friend since 1978)

"Brian Doyle, a Major League Player, is a Major League Christian, a Major League husband, a Major League dad, a Major League brother, a Major League friend, a Major League teacher, a Major League encourager and played in the Majors with the New York Yankees. If you want to be a Major League anything, this is the book for you."

-Bible Actor Mac McConnell

"Meeting Brian as a student at Doyle Baseball School changed me. His passion for Jesus and baseball transformed my life and career. Thirty years later I was challenged again by reading THE CALL. Thank you, Brian!"

-Christopher Hudson
Author and former Head Softball Coach at Wheaton College

"What a pleasure to read about the life of my dear friend Brian Doyle and to know that you do not need to worry, and you need not fear! A man who has removed the veil and shown us how joy does come in the morning."

-Susan Gaines
Editor and Ghostwriter

The Call

THE CALL

THE DESIRE TO FINISH STRONG

"THE CALL is a must read. Destiny connected Brian and me as teammates and brothers in Christ. His legacy of faith and hope through many obstacles will give you encouragement to finish strong. Enjoy reading this great book of hope." - Willie Randolph, Former NY Yankee 2nd Baseman

BRIAN DOYLE
1978 WORLD SERIES CHAMPION

GLOBAL PUBLISHING

Global Publishing
2301 Lucien Way #415
Maitland, FL 32751
407.339.4217
www.xulonpress.com

© 2019 by Brian Doyle

All rights reserved solely by the author. The author guarantees all contents are original and do not infringe upon the legal rights of any other person or work. No part of this book may be reproduced in any form without the permission of the author. The views expressed in this book are not necessarily those of the publisher.

Unless otherwise indicated, scripture quotations are taken from The New King James Version. Copyright 1979, 1980, 1982 by Thomas Nelson, Inc.

The HOLY BIBLE, NEW INTERNATIONAL VERSION,. (NIV) Copyright © 1973, 1978, 1984 by International Bible Society. and The Holy Bible, King James Version. Copyright © 1972 by Thomas Nelson Inc., Camden, New Jersey 08103. Used by permission. All right reserved. Printed in the United States of America.

ISBN-13: 978-1-54565-737-9

Acknowledgments

To Tom Wright, thank you for dreaming with me and encouraging me years ago to write my autobiography, *The Call*.

To Susan Gaines, thank you for being the first editor and the first teacher to coach me how to go about writing this autobiography. I couldn't have done it without your guidance.

To Trevor Hamaker, thank you for your part in editing and for being such a wonderful, godly husband and father to my daughter and to my grandchildren.

To my family, Kirk and Amy, Parker, Payton, and Paris, Kristin and Trevor, Tyson, and Reagan for patiently listening as I read my drafts to you for your feedback. I am so thrilled this is all documented for my children, grandchildren, and generations to come. I am thrilled and thankful that you all are my arrows of light in this world. I love you.

Larry Keefauver, thank you for being the professional editor of this book. You have been an answer to our prayers.

Alice Wright and Vicki Rose, thank you for being our unofficial editors. Susan "Gussie" Branstetter, thank you for making a final read for us and helping to find a couple of KY corrections that only our childhood and lifelong friend could find.

Thank you, Jeff Siegel, for being my accountability partner for well over twenty years. Thank you for knowing my soul. Thank you for being such a great friend and God's hand to help me finish this process. I know that we will continue to turn spiritual double plays for JESUS.

My dear Connie, the love of my life since I was seventeen years old. I have told her hundreds of times and have told hundreds of people that she is the best person that I have ever known. Without her love this book would not have been written. She took over and made this book a reality with many hours of editing, phone calls, blood, sweat, and tears!

Acknowledgments

Connie, I love you with all my heart and thank you for loving me. You are my godly wife, mother of our beautiful adult kiddos, and my best friend. Thank you.

Foreword

"The Original Natural"

Years ago, I saw the movie "The Natural" about a mythical baseball player who beat the odds and brought his team the world championship. . . .

Did I say "mythical"? Oh, that was before I met Brian Doyle. . .the true "Natural" and one of the greatest individuals I have ever met in my lifetime. Brian is the one who will always beat the odds. He will overcome any obstacle in life. It would be a mistake to say "never" to this giant. His deep faith will always provide his heart and life with abundant hope. Why?

The Call

Because Brian Doyle ALWAYS answered THE CALL.

- He answered the call to become one of the legends associated with the greatest baseball team in professional sports…THE NEW YORK YANKEES.
- He answered the call to be a great husband and loving father, grandfather, mentor, and friend.
- He answered the call to face a life-threatening disease and refused to allow this opponent to record the "win"!
- However, all this is possible because Brian Doyle truly answered The Call; the call to commit his life to JESUS CHRIST; and the call to serve Him passionately… regardless of what field in life he may be playing.

As in his professional life as a baseball player, Brian brings an even greater passion when he is talking to people about his faith. Once you meet Brian, you will never forget the encounter. He will love you, he will encourage you, he will have you laughing one minute and crying the next.

Foreword

But this one thing I promise from your encounter with Brian Doyle, he will ALWAYS tell you the most important decision in your life is to "Answer the Call!" Not from the Yankees, but from the real BOSS! JESUS CHRIST.

"The Call" is not only entertaining, it is challenging, uplifting, and inspirational. As you read these pages, you will feel as if Brian is your best friend. But here's the secret. He has the capacity to love everyone as if they are his best friend. This book is not just the carefully crafted stories of Brian Doyle's life. IT IS BRIAN DOYLE'S LOVE AND HIS PASSION THAT CHALLENGES AND INSPIRES EVERY READER!

I love Brian Doyle! I'm honored to know his life and even more humbled to know the man. I am eternally thankful that God brought Brian and Connie into our lives and now I am thankful he will be a part of your life as you read his inspiring story! God bless you and I encourage you to follow Brian's example and "Answer the Call!"

-Dr. Larry L. Thompson, Pastor Emeritus,
First Baptist Church of Fort Lauderdale

The Call

From the humble fields of Kentucky to Baseball's Field of Champions, Brian's inspirational success story is the quintessential American promise - stay true to your dreams, work hard, persevere, and you will be ready when opportunity calls.

Brian's life story reads like a great novel or Hollywood script, rich with action and life's challenges – no, it isn't from the creative mind of an author or screenwriter, Brian lived it!

As a longtime friend, I continue to admire and appreciate Brian for his many loves: his high school sweetheart and bride of forty-five years, Connie; his family; his friends; and his Lord.

Despite all the physical challenges of sports, health, and the temptations of fame, he remained true to his ideals, which is rare in these days of instant everything.

Our friendship began when my wife and I began attending a neighborhood Bible study that Brian and Connie led. Shortly thereafter, I was diagnosed with throat cancer and had to have surgery. Although only newly acquainted, Brian and Connie accompanied my wife and me to the hospital and remained there for moral support for over four hours. Thus, began my battle against cancer,

Foreword

our faith journey, and an enduring friendship with Brian and Connie.

As you will read, one major challenge for Brian was overcoming Leukemia which brought him to the threshold of death. God used this challenge to equip him and give him a burden for ministering to cancer patients specifically and hospital patients in general. This became one of his many duties as an ordained minister at First Baptist Church, Fort Lauderdale, Florida. As a pastor, Brian came into his own with a gift of evangelism. His boldness and faith allowed him to lead literally hundreds around the world to Jesus Christ - from the mission field of South Florida and beyond to the international outreach of the First Baptist Church Christmas Pageant. The worldwide baseball ministry, Global Baseball, allowed him to access the lost in Communist and Muslim countries, leading many to Christ including dignitaries.

As you read Brian's story, you will be inspired knowing that with faith, family and friends, much is possible, even probable for those who believe!

-Tom Wright
Servant Leader Ministry,
First Baptist Church, Fort Lauderdale

Table of Contents

Introduction - The Call xxvii

Chapter 1 - The Call: One More Push 33

Chapter 2 - The Call: To Adventure 39

Chapter 3 - The Call: To Play Up 43

Chapter 4 - The Call: Dad Is Dying 49

Chapter 5 - The Call: To Dream 55

Chapter 6 - The Call: Can They Play Up? 60

Chapter 7 - The Call: Knee Surgery and
No Front Teeth 71

Chapter 8 - The Call: I Know Who I Am to Marry 78

Chapter 9 - The Call: You Can't Play Football 85

Chapter 10 - The Call: Texas Rangers 96

Chapter 11 - The Call: I'm Going to Be a Father 108

Chapter 12 - The Call: Traded to the Yankees 118

Chapter 13 - The Call: To Repentance! 124

The Call

Chapter 14 - Connie Made The Call 130

Chapter 15 - The Call: "Doyle Second Base" 137

Chapter 16 - The Call: To Win 145

Chapter 17 - The Call: Can I Play? 158

Chapter 18 - The Call: To Evangelize 173

Chapter 19 - The Call: Doyle Baseball 178

Chapter 20 - The Call: To Be a Husband 191

Chapter 21 - The Call: To Make Followers
of Jesus 200

Chapter 22 - The Call: Is a Free Agent
Really Free? 207

Chapter 23 - The Call: Let's Do it All! 219

Chapter 24 - Discovering Who I Am Is
Not About What I Do 234

Chapter 25 - The Call: Doctor Says Cancer 238

Chapter 26 - The Call: You Have Six Months 243

Chapter 27 - The Call to God: Protect Them 249

Chapter 28 - The Call: Downsize to Build Up 252

Chapter 29 - The Call: It's a Brand-New Game 259

Chapter 30 - The Call: I Had to Answer 262

Chapter 31 - The Call: Obeyed at Age 50 265

Chapter 32 - The Call Out: God Help! 268

Table of Contents

Chapter 33 - The Call: Safe at Home 275

Chapter 34 - The Call: Mission Work 281

Chapter 35 - The Call: Parkinson's Disease 290

Chapter 36 - The Call: Brian Doyle Day? 295

Chapter 37 - The Call: From the Batter's Box
to Home 300

Chapter 38 - The Call: Finish Strong 304

INTRODUCTION

The Call

There are important decisions a person needs to make before engaging in any sport or game. One of mine began at the age of forty.

My joints were so painful I decided to visit a friend of mine, Dr. Bruce Clement, a rheumatologist. Prior to this, I'd had pneumonia and months of symptoms that led to visiting several doctors. Dr. Clement ordered a blood workup, which no one else had done. The very next morning at 8 a.m., my phone rang.

Dr. Clement said, "Brian, I need to see you."

I asked him when and he said, "Now, before anyone gets to my office."

> **I got "The Call."**

The Call

I quickly told my brothers, Denny and Blake, that Dr. Clement needed to see me right away and left. When I walked into his office, I could see that Bruce had been crying. It is not good when your doctor is crying while trying to tell you what is wrong.

He said my blood work came back and he was sure I had cancer. He told me he had no way of knowing what kind, but that my blood was in bad shape. He had already called Moffitt Cancer Center in Tampa, Florida, to set up an appointment for the very next morning.

I walked out of his office, unlocked my car, and sat down with my feet still outside of the car.

I said, "Father, if this is what I have to go through, I ask You to take care of Connie and help my son, Kirk, and my daughter, Kristin, know You more intimately than I have known You."

Then I put my feet in the car, laid my head back, and cried out, "Father, is this what it boils down to?"

God spoke louder than an audible voice and said, "Son, it is what it is always about; you either trust Me or you don't."

The Call

At that moment, I felt the peace that passes all understanding. Knowing I was in the presence of the Lord, I started to pray for myself.

The Holy Spirit very loudly said, "You are not to pray for yourself."

> **Now that's a wakeup CALL.**

Wow, was that a curve ball! There I was knowing I had some kind of cancer and I was not to pray for myself?

The Holy Spirit said again, "You either trust Me or you don't."

I went home and told my wife Connie the situation and explained we needed to go to the Moffitt Center the next morning. Needless to say, she was in a state of shock, confusion, and helplessness. I tried to empathize with her, asking myself how I would have acted if the roles were reversed.

We went to Moffitt Cancer Center that next morning. We waited less than thirty minutes and then I was taken to an examination room.

A female doctor walked in, introduced herself, and said, "I am the physician who will be executing your bone tap."

The Call

I thought, *"Wait a minute, this is the first thing that is going to happen? I don't know anything about a bone tap."* I asked her to explain what she was about to do. She said she was going into my bone and extract bone marrow for testing. She said she would go through the sternum or my hip and get the marrow. I chose my hip. She would start by giving me a local in the right side of the small of my lower back. Knowing this was my first bone marrow tap, she said she would give me something to bite on. Then she instructed me to remain perfectly still and hold on to the top legs of the table.

Being a macho man, I said, "No problem, let's get this show on the road."

The local was a piece of cake. Then she hammered (that's right, you read it correctly) she hammered a sharp steel tube into my body, which hit bone. She hammered and hammered. I kept biting and holding onto the table legs.

She said, "I hate working on you athletes because you have the hardest bones."

At the time, there was no way for me to apologize. In fact, I just wanted to scream, "Hurry up!" She finally broke through and put a long syringe down the tube to draw out the marrow.

It was only a few seconds later when she said, "Sorry, Mr. Doyle, we hit a dry socket. We will have to try another spot."

Hit a dry socket? Try another spot? Are you kidding me? She said it like she had just gone down the wrong aisle of a grocery store to find a product, but no worries there are more aisles. I could feel the sweat dripping from her head.

She gave me a breather, so I asked her how many of these procedures she did a day. Her answer was only four or five because it was so taxing physically. I had no sympathy for her.

Then, once again she gave me a local to numb the area. I bit down and held on to the table as she started hammering away again.

I heard her say to herself, "Finally." I said to myself, "Thank God!" She put the syringe down the tube and drew out the marrow. She asked me to lie there for a minute and she would be right back. She returned in less than a minute and handed me a towel to wipe the sweat off my face. Then she directed me to another room where Connie was waiting.

The Call

Dr. Spiers came into the room, pulled his chair right up in front of me, and said I had *Hairy Cell Leukemia*. Connie asked him what stage. He said that it didn't matter because I needed chemotherapy right away.

> **This book is about THE CALL and how it influenced my life.**

"Excuse me," I said. "My wife just asked you a question and you need to answer her."

He told us that I was in the final stage and had approximately six months to live.

Line Drive

*When you are in a situation where you have no control, you better know the real Jesus. When you feel helpless, you must realize only God is your refuge and strength and an ever-present help in time of trouble (Psalm 46:1). When you need hope, you need to understand that **He** is your hope.*

I felt that hope in spite of what the doctor said as I was bathed in His peace that surpasses all understanding.

CHAPTER 1

The Call: One More Push

Identical twins were born to Robert and Virginia Doyle on January 26, 1954, in a small conservative town in the heart of Kentucky situated just between Louisville and Nashville, Tennessee. Really it is between Chicken Bristle, Cub Run, Uno, Bear Wallow, and Knob Lick. There was only one traffic light, but many family-owned motels peppered the main street whose signs read, "Sleep, Eat, Swim Now." It was "Cave Country" with Mammoth Cave National Park only a few miles away.

Mother was forty-two and Dad was forty-three when they were shocked by the news they were expecting a baby. They were even more shocked when the doctor said to keep pushing after the birth of the first child because there was another. The doctor had no clue that Mom was pregnant with twins. Not only were mom and dad shocked, their thirteen-year-old daughter, Janice, and eleven-year-old son, Dennis (nicknamed Denny), were as well.

Which one is which?
(I have bigger eyes and always ready for action)

Loving each other from the beginning

Having an identical twin was so much fun because when one of us had an adventurous idea, we would act upon it. Blake and I were also very fortunate to grow up having an older sister and brother, Janice and Denny. They took us everywhere they went; they had to.

It became even cooler during their high school years. We were always a part of their lives whether they liked it or not. We learned to keep our mouths shut and just look and listen. Needless to say, we were a little wiser about things than our peers. Even at a very young age, we thought that we could do just about anything because we had watched and learned from Denny and Janice's high school experiences.

When it came to athletics, I always had a partner to practice and play with me. I also had a partner when one of us was naughty. It did not matter what happened, Mom and Dad did not even ask who did this or that. They assumed we both were involved and we both got a spanking.

We never knew Dad's mother and father. They both died before we were born. However, we did have a great-grandmother, Mama Toohey, who we saw every week. I never saw her standing or sitting; she was always in her bed. She chewed tobacco and had a spittoon on the floor next to the bed. Blake and I thought it was awesome that she never missed. However, kissing her goodbye was not as awesome.

Our Papa Toohey, my mom's dad, took care of great-grandmother, Mama Toohey. He stayed in the little three-room house after she passed. There was a living room, a bedroom, and a kitchen. It had electricity, but did not have running water or a bathroom. The well was 15 yards from the house and the outhouse was 25 yards from the house.

The side yard of this "mansion" was a very large garden. When it was planting time, we would stay with Papa and help him plant the seeds. Name it and we planted it. I will never forget the time Papa told us to weed the garden, but he didn't show us what the weeds looked like compared to the potatoes. When he came back to check on us, Blake and I had pulled

We grew up in those early years always being with high school and college student athletes.

up all the potatoes. Man, did we get a whooping! We learned what the leaves of a potato plant looked like after that.

Growing up, we traveled to athletic events and college basketball and baseball games with our sister and brother. Janice was a cheerleader for Western Kentucky University and Denny was a basketball and baseball player for Morehead State University. Our experiences were amazing for young boys from a small town.

At six years old, we were shagging baseballs for Dennis Doyle and Joe Campbell, two future Major League Baseball players. Dennis started with the Philadelphia Phillies and Joe with the Chicago Cubs. Both Denny and Joe went to Morehead State University. When the team would go on their spring trip south, they would stop and pick up Blake and me to be the bat boys for the Morehead State University Eagles.

Line Drive

"Your beginnings will seem humble, so prosperous will your future be" (Job 8:7 NIV). Each and every one of us has our steps ordered by the

Lord. Little did I know my beginning was so planned by God that it would take me to such an adventurous life.

Adventure is just around the corner for everyone, though not many are willing to stick their neck out to take it. We need to remember the only way a turtle moves forward is by sticking his neck out.

In Matthew 13:24-30, Jesus told a parable about a field of wheat where weeds were also growing. The weeds look just like wheat. My brother and I did not know the difference between the potatoes and weeds.

Jesus wants us to be the fruit producers. To effectively do that we need to know the difference between the fruit and the weeds.

CHAPTER 2

The Call: To Adventure

At nine months, we were walking and experiencing all kinds of mischievous moments (I mean adventures). When we were thirteen months old, Mom and Dad were building a four-bedroom house by themselves. We decided to paint the new sheetrock walls with wood stain. We were scolded and decided to leave the house, so we would be safe from more scolding. You see, by now, we had our own identical twin language. Even the doctor was puzzled at how easy it was for us to communicate. Venturing out of the house in our diapers and t-shirts on a very cool morning in September, we wielded our toy rifle pop-guns just in case the adventure found trouble.

The Call

Several blocks from home, four dogs saw twin toddlers and came running toward us. With no confidence in the rifles we were holding, we quickly dropped our weapons and ran. Screaming, crying, running, and panicked, we ended up at a lady's house several blocks away. The woman took us in her arms and called our Mom and Dad. The ever-present loud voice of adventure was always in one of our heads, and whoever heard it, was eager to share with the other. The "call" to adventure was constantly heard.

Everything we did was a competition. It did not matter if it was cleaning windows at the house. By the way, we had a picture window in the front of the house that had ninety-six little window panes. I think they should be named "window pains." Whether it was playing a sport or mowing the lawn, we competed. We never got upset with each other about winning or losing. It was a natural thing because there were two of us.

We were so close in our relationship that if one of us made a grade of 100 percent and the other 96 percent, then on the next test, one of us

> **Adventure is a good thing when you are prepared.**

would miss one question or math problem on purpose in order for us to have the same grades.

When the doctor told my mom she wasn't finished and to give one more push, that push brought into the world quite an adventure for a forty-two-year-old mom and a forty-three-year-old dad.

We lived in an area that is famous for caves. In fact, Mammoth Cave National Park is just a few miles from our house. Blake and I would go "caving," which to us was to see the mouth of a cave and go into it. That adventurous spirit didn't always find us in a pleasant situation. We would find Native American Indian arrow heads that excited us, but we would also find animal bones which really scared us.

Line Drive

I love adventure! Sometimes it is not pleasant, especially if we aren't prepared. Sometimes we have to go through it to give life.

Is there something in your life today that needs "one more push"?

Is there something that needs life that has been dormant for a long time?

The Holy Spirit knows what it is. Ask Him and He will not only tell you, He will help you. Why? Because the main job of the Holy Spirit is to exalt the name of Jesus. By going through the adventure, Jesus will be exalted, and all the glory will and should go to Him.

CHAPTER 3

The Call: To Play Up

Since the age of five, our parents kept us busy and involved in sports. The backyard of our home became the neighborhood baseball field. All the boys in the neighborhood came to play. Anything that could keep us busy with a ball was the perfect activity to squelch the call to adventure. Structure and discipline were the main ideas for the home ball games and we loved it. Plus, it kept us right at home.

If we didn't play at home, we walked to the Davis' house where they had a large field in the back of their house that sloped up about twenty feet to where we lived. Next door to the field was the lumber yard. We could go during a break and buy a Coca Cola for 5 cents out of the machine they had in the lobby.

Now, I want you to understand that we would play baseball from 8:00 a.m. until dark or dinner. We did stop for lunch, went home, and ate. It also gave us a chance to beg for a nickel, so we could buy another Coca Cola. Then everyone would return, and we'd start the game right where we left it. Mrs. Mayme Davis was usually the umpire. She had a son Carl who was one year older than me. Playing with older boys always helped us improve our skills. Carl's sister, Mayme Lou, was very brave and would grab her glove and join the game, until she received two black eyes. She became our cheerleader after that!

Dad would go to the lumber yard and get scrap 2" by 4" scrap wood and bent 16 penny nails (large, thick nails). He would bring them home and Blake and I would straighten the nails. Dad had a six-ounce and an eight-ounce hammer. He had us place our

> **With consistent practice and a constant playmate, we quickly became athletic with exceptional hand-eye coordination.**

elbows on the ground and hammer those nails into the wood with our forearms and wrist. Dad told us that the four sports we played—baseball, basketball, football, and tennis—all required strong grips and forearms.

We also had much fun in our basement. There was no heat or air conditioning, but it didn't need it. The walls were lined with cinder blocks and there was three feet between them and the ground. Dad built a ping pong table for us. He said it was great for hand-eye coordination.

The very first sport Dad taught us was tennis. Blake and I would walk the half mile to the courts and play for hours if there weren't enough boys to play baseball. Dad told us if we could play tennis well, we could play any sport. He was right again. Tennis improved footwork and hand-eye coordination and developed strong grips and strong forearms.

One day, Dad made "the call" and said it was time for us to get involved in organized sports. Dad became the coach of an eight- to ten-year-old baseball team, which was part of a recreational league made up of two towns, Cave City and Horse Cave. Having the authority of a head coach, he drafted his twin five-year-old sons onto the team. The other coaches in the league gladly allowed him to take two spots in the draft even though it was an eight- to ten-year-old league.

Mom dressed us exactly alike every day, so the uniforms that we wore for baseball were great. They looked just the same. The only problem was our numbers weren't the same, but at least the front of the uniforms matched.

My First Official Game

Before the first game, Dad said, "Boys, come and sit down. There are some important decisions that you need to make before you play your first game. These two decisions do not take talent, but they do need to be made. The first decision is that when you are up at the plate, you must make the decision to swing at every pitch. You do not have time to decide if the pitch is a ball or a strike. You do have the time to stop your swing. So, are you going to swing the bat at every pitch?"

We answered him, "Yes, Sir."

"The next decision that you will have to make," Dad continued, "is you never, ever, allow the umpire to call you out on the third strike. You have to make that decision.

Do not give the other team a free out. When you have two strikes as a hitter you must be over aggressive. If the pitch is close enough for the umpire to call it a strike, it is close enough for you to hit it. Are you going to make the decision that you will never, ever, allow the umpire to call you out on the third strike?"

We again answered, "Yes, Sir."

We were so excited, it was our very first official game. Dad put me in center field. I was so excited and nervous that I wet my pants. I had to run home to change into regular pants, but because I was then out of uniform, I could not play my very first game. I was devastated.

The next week during practice, Dad had me try out for shortstop. I won the position. Now I was going to play my first game as a shortstop. I ran out to the field to my position. Mom walked up and sat in a folding chair. I was so proud and excited that I began waving to Mom. The pitcher was taking his warm-up pitches and Dad walked out to me.

He stooped over and said, "Son, the game is played on the field, not in the stands. Go and take a seat."

Again, I missed playing my very first official game. Since that day, I have never looked in the stands to see who was there.

> *We all are called to play up sometime in our lives.*

Finally, I got to play my first game. I wasn't nervous, and I did not look up in the stands or outside of the fence. Dad had taught us how to drag bunt. Being only five-year-olds, he had made sure that we could succeed in playing against eight-, nine-, and ten-year-old boys. We were very fast runners and were very successful in getting on base. It was so much fun to play organized baseball.

Line Drive

When was the last time that the call came for you to play up? Was it to visit someone in the hospital or someone to share the Gospel with in your neighborhood? Maybe it was God who called you to give some money to a ministry, but at the time it would really have been a sacrifice.

CHAPTER 4

The Call: Dad Is Dying

One evening a year later, we were in the back seat of our Oldsmobile while Dad was taking Mom to a friend's house. Dad, Blake, and I waited outside while Mom dropped a package off to her friend. Mom walked out of the house and Dad tried to start the car, but it would not start. Dad got out of the car and started pushing it. As it rolled, he jumped back in the driver's seat and it started.

We were off for home, but a mile down the road Dad started getting chest pains. We stopped at the local Dairy Queen and Mom ran in to call the doctor. A young man came out with Mom, and he got in the driver's seat and drove Dad to the doctor's office. In what seemed only minutes, an ambulance came by and took Dad to the hospital, twelve miles away.

Then the call came. The doctor wanted us to go in to see Dad for the last time. We walked in to see our Dad lying in a hospital bed with some kind of mask on his face. Mom said it was an oxygen mask. We knew that Dad was going to die and go to heaven, but we were confused. We didn't talk to each other. We didn't know what to say. We would sit in the car for what seemed like hours by ourselves. Mom wanted us protected from it all. About every hour, Janice or Denny would come out and check on us.

We listened to our older siblings and other adults discuss our Dad's situation, but it didn't make sense to us. A month passed, and Dad was sent home. We decided that the doctor didn't know what he was talking about. However, Dad was not the big muscular man that we knew. He was now skinny and walked very slowly, but we didn't mind because we finally had our Dad home.

Elementary school was just starting, and Dad got a job as the janitor, because he could no longer do the physically taxing job of building homes. We would get up each morning in the winter at 4:00 a.m. and go with Dad to the school. There we would shovel coal into the two furnaces to heat up the two school buildings. Afterward, we would head home and Dad would make a big breakfast. We did this task all through our elementary school years.

We got jobs in the summer and fall to help our family financially. Kentucky being a huge tobacco state, we went to family and friends who raised tobacco seeking work. Being paid by the row, we made money by priming tobacco, which was done on our hands and knees. We had to pull off the bottom leaves and then hang the leaves up in the barn. We also hauled in hay bales. That wasn't a bit fun. Mom did not believe in blue jeans for her boys. She had us wear polyester slacks. Our thighs would have scrapes and cuts because the hay straws would penetrate our pants and our skin.

Dad was getting healthier and Mom got a job at the local drug store. We continued playing football, basketball, and baseball with Mom and Dad never missing a practice or a game. Athletics were still a big part of the family.

As we got older, we started cleaning the upstairs of the school's classrooms, hallways, and bathrooms. Dad was not allowed to walk up the stairs because of his heart condition. I will never forget the afternoon we came downstairs and told Dad that we were finished.

He asked, "Did you do a very good job?"

We answered, "Yes."

Then he said that we were to go to each classroom and write our names on the chalkboard saying we had cleaned this room. Immediately, we stated that we were not quite done yet. That was a meaningful experience.

> **Ever since then, whatever I did I would ask myself if I would be satisfied enough to put my name on it.**

I will never forget the afternoon that we were cleaning the upstairs classrooms and the English teacher, Mrs. Ruth Saunders, came screaming out of her classroom, yelling for my Dad. She ran down the stairs and we followed, wondering what was going on.

She kept yelling, "Jake!" which was Dad's nickname. Dad came out of a room he was cleaning. Mrs. Saunders quickly gave Dad a note she had found and said we had to do something quickly. It read, "Some "N—" are going to be at the gym, let's go shoot some."

Caverna was the first high school in the state of Kentucky to be integrated. Dad had to put his hand over his mouth to hide the fact he was grinning. The note meant that there were some black guys at the gym playing basketball and some of the other guys wanted to shoot some baskets with them. Dad quickly calmed Mrs. Saunders down and explained that the note did not mean what she thought it meant.

Line Drive

Dad asked the Lord in the hospital to allow him to see his boys grow up. The Lord granted his request. Dad made sure that we knew that.

So it is with each of us. Each of us must die to live. That is the life that only Jesus can give because He is the Way, the Truth, and the Life. We need to let people know that He granted us our request to make Him Lord and grants us everlasting life.

If I asked you to confess, where would your mind take you? I would bet it took you to confess some sin. The Bible uses the word confess five times more in confessing Jesus as Lord. So, let's think about that for a few seconds. If we are confessing Jesus as Lord most of our time during the day, I know that there would be less sin to confess. Think about it. If you know Him as Lord, your name is written in the Lamb's Book of Life, on His "chalkboard" in His Father's house where there are many rooms.

Can we at least write the name of Jesus on our tongues so that His name is proclaimed throughout our world of influence? If not, then we need to go back and clean up what we skipped the first time just like Blake and I had to do. Then we can write our name on the chalkboard.

CHAPTER 5

The Call: To Dream

I vividly remember a day Blake and I made a baseball field out of a plowed-under corn field in the back of our house. We had measured the bases and cut cardboard bases out of boxes to make them seem as real as possible. I was nine years old sitting on that second base looking out at the forest in the outfield. I was dreaming that I was playing in Yankee Stadium. The trees were blowing in the wind, and I was

> **My dream came true and so can yours.**

imagining that they were fans going crazy after I knocked in a run. I got up from that cardboard second base and ran to touch the cardboard third base and slid into the cardboard home plate.

It was 1963 and the Yankees were my favorite team. Mickey Mantle, Roger Maris, Whitey Ford, Yogi Berra, Bobby Richardson, and Tony Kubek were just a few of my favorite players.

> **The largest nation in the world is your imagination.**

I slid into that cardboard home plate, stood up, dusted myself off, and jogged into the ditch next to the gravel road, believing it was the real Yankee Stadium dugout. Mickey, Roger, Whitey, Yogi, Tony, and Bobby were patting me on the backside saying, "Nice going, kid."

I loved wrapping myself in my imagination, because I believed in myself and knew if I worked hard enough those things I imagined would come true.

Fifteen Years Later

I am at the plate and hit a line drive to center field. A runner is on second base. The throw goes to the plate and the runner is safe. I advanced to second base. The crowd is going crazy because I just knocked in the tying run. There

I am standing on the real Yankee Stadium second base with tears trickling down my cheeks. Davey Lopes, the LA Dodgers second baseman, and Bill Russell, the shortstop, are looking at me with very peculiar faces. I'm not crying because I just knocked Lou Pinella in for the tying run, I'm crying because I am remembering a nine-year-old boy sitting on a cardboard second base in a plowed-under cornfield just between the towns of Chicken Bristle, Bear Wallow, Cub Run, Uno, and Knob Lick.

Bucky Dent was the next batter up and he hit a ball into left field. I rounded and stepped on the real Yankee Stadium third base and slid into the real Yankee Stadium home plate. I popped up to my feet and jogged into the real Yankee Dugout where Reggie Jackson, Thurman Munson, Jim "Catfish" Hunter, Roy White, Goose Gossage, Chris Chambliss, and Mickey Rivers patted me on my backside and said, "Nice going, kid."

The All-Star Team

I also remember well when we were eleven years old, Dad and some other men thought the four teams from Cave City and Horse Cave had enough good players among them that could go to Lexington and play in the state tournament for eleven- and twelve-year olds. So, the coaches picked an all-star team from the four teams. Just about everyone from our sand lot games was on the team.

When we got to Lexington, Kentucky, we all stayed in old army barracks. The very first day we went to the field just to look at it. We were amazed that it had grass on the infield. We had never played on a grass infield.

Dad told us all to go sit in the stands. An older man came up and stood in front of us. Dad introduced him to us. It was Earl Combs. He had played for the New York Yankees and was inducted into the Major League Baseball Hall of Fame. Mr. Combs talked for about ten minutes.

I don't remember anything he said except, "Boys, you don't know, maybe one of you will play professional baseball."

Well, he underestimated. Three boys on that team did play professional baseball: me, Blake, and Dennis Rock. We also won the State Championship.

Earl Combs took me closer to my dream. I had met a real New York Yankee.

Line Drive

You see, if my dreams can come true, why can't yours? I am still dreaming. My imagination is still vivid. Whether you are nine or ninety, you are not really living unless you are dreaming!

Psalm 37:4-5 reminds us, "Delight yourself in the Lord and He will give you the desires of your heart. Commit your ways to Him, trust also in Him, and He will do it. (NKJV)"

Maybe my dreaming was a lot stronger than Mr. Combs.

CHAPTER 6

The Call: Can They Play Up?

When we got to junior high school, Dad got the job as janitor of the junior and senior high school building. After school or after practice, Blake, Mom, and I would clean the upstairs of the school building while Dad, who couldn't walk up stairs because of his heart, cleaned the first floor.

> **At thirteen years old, I was playing High School Varsity Baseball.**

Blake and I would practice basketball after cleaning the upstairs classrooms and restrooms. Dad was an excellent basketball teacher. He was a very good player on his high school team in Cave City. He also had received a scholarship to attend the University of Kentucky. The Kentucky team was called the "Fab Five." They not only won the NCAA Division 1 Championship, they won the Olympics.

Dad chose to stay home, become a carpenter, get married, and his little family expanded. He was masterful at his teaching. He put paper around sunglasses and put them on us, so we couldn't see and had us dribble the basketball with both hands. We practiced constantly handling the ball, passing the ball, and shooting. Blake and I became the starting guards of the seventh and eighth grade teams.

Dad continued to coach us in the summer baseball league in his quiet, encouraging way. I will never forget a game when Blake was on third base and one of our teammates hit a ball that went foul down the right field line. The first baseman caught the ball and Blake tagged up and scored.

The umpire was very loud while throwing his hands up, screaming, "The run does not count, go back to third base."

The Call

Dad walked up to the umpire and asked why the runner had to go back to third base? The umpire quickly and loudly stated that a runner cannot score on a foul ball. Dad did not argue and had Blake go back to third. Eventually, Blake scored.

I was the pitcher in that game. As I was throwing my warm-up pitches, Dad walked up to me and asked for the ball.

I asked Dad, "Are you taking me out of the game?"

He said no and walked down to home plate with the ball. There he bent over and with his finger drew a big circle in front of the plate. Then he walked back about ten feet toward the mound and with his foot made a straight line.

The umpire came out to Dad and asked, "Jake, what in the world are you doing?"

Dad calmly answered, "Well, I thought that we would play a game of marbles. Maybe you would know the rules of that game."

The umpire did not throw Dad out of the game because he knew Dad knew the rules of baseball better than he did. All the fans were snickering. I wanted to bust out laughing, but I held it in. What a way to get the point across. After he made that statement, Dad flipped me the ball and the game continued.

Fun Becomes Fear

Then came the call in January. The new varsity baseball coach called Dad and asked if Blake and I could try out for the varsity baseball team as eighth graders. Dad told the coach yes. We were so excited. We made the varsity baseball team, Blake starting at second base and me at third base.

Playing in a varsity sport in the eighth grade is hard on everyone. The upper classmen did not like it one bit that two junior high kids were starting for the varsity. We were surrounded by upper classmen, beaten up, placed in wire lockers, and urinated upon. A few days later, Dad's tires were slashed. I started dreading going to school every single day knowing kids would be scheming how to hurt me.

Fun became fear.

It was extremely tough. However, Blake and I learned that we were strong together. We vowed that we would never be caught without one another to defend ourselves. We became proficient in backing down the older boys. That would sound like a very positive thing. However, it brought into me both pride and cockiness. Being able to back down the "big boys" gave me an arrogance that I should not have had. Plus, I relied on Blake being with me. If I was by myself, it would not have been that way. So, fun became fear, fear became arrogance. Do you know anyone who likes people that are arrogant? I don't.

Blake played second base and I played third base. I remember playing in the conference tournament in Greensburg, Kentucky. A play came to me and I was ready to tag the runner out. This large guy ran me over. I was knocked back a good ten yards, but I held onto the ball and the guy was out.

After the inning, Dad came to the bench and told me, "The next time that happens just step to the side, take the ball into your bare hand and tag the guy in the mouth." Sure enough, just a few innings

> **A few years later, though, I would reap what I sowed. . . missing a lot of teeth!**

The Call: Can They Play Up?

later the same thing happened only with another player. I tagged the guy out by putting the ball right in his mouth. It took a while to get the guy up, minus a few teeth. No one tried to run me over the rest of the tournament.

Blake became the Batting Champion as an eighth grader on the Varsity Team. The High School Athletic Banquet was scheduled and "the call" came to our Dad. Because we were under classmen, we could not attend the Athletic Banquet at the high school. Though Dad was a quiet man, when he spoke, he spoke with a purpose. He told the Athletic Director that if his boys were not to be considered to have earned a "Varsity Letter" for playing varsity baseball and if the state of Kentucky would not recognize they were on a varsity roster, then they could transfer to any high school in the area and not have to lay out a year.

The rule in Kentucky was that if you transferred to another high school and did not live in the same district, you had to lay out one full season before becoming eligible to play that sport. The Athletic Director quickly told Dad that the boys could attend the banquet and earn a letter. The funny thing is, the call came to Dad from another

The Call

high school's Athletic Director, who will remain nameless, just a few weeks earlier offering Dad a good paying job. In addition to that job offer, this man stated that when we turned sixteen, we each could have a Ford Mustang in the color of our choice. Dad declined that offer.

However, at the Athletic Banquet, Blake would not receive the Batting Champion trophy because he was an underclassman. Dad was okay with that, because trophies were not that important to him. During the banquet, Coach Coy Meadows did recognize Blake as having the highest batting average. The trophy went to the second highest average player, who was a senior on the team. The next four years I beat Blake out of the Batting Champion honor by no more than .002. Ha, ha, Blake.

That summer our brother Denny was playing in the Major Leagues with the Philadelphia Phillies. The Phillies were coming to Cincinnati to play the Reds. We were so excited because it would be our first time to see Denny playing live. We drove from our little Kentucky home to Cincinnati. We checked into the hotel where the Phillies were staying. A few minutes later, Denny knocked on the door and there were hugs all around.

The Call: Can They Play Up?

After a few moments, Denny declared that he had a surprise for Blake and me. The manager of the Phillies, Frank Lucchesi, brought two extra uniforms. We were going to take infield and batting practice with the Phillies. The only stipulation that Denny gave us was that we were not to ask for any autographs when we got into the stadium. Denny got a cab and the three of us were off to Riverfront Stadium.

When the taxi stopped to let us out, a car came screeching by and made a left turn into a parking lot. I couldn't believe my eyes. It was Pete Rose, the icon of the Reds. I had put the hotel notepad and pen in my back pants pocket, ignoring the rule Denny had given us. Besides, we weren't in the stadium yet.

I sprinted into the parking lot and said, "Mr. Rose, may I please have your autograph?"

He quickly barked, "Get lost, kid!"

I was devastated, heartbroken, embarrassed, and chastised by Denny.

The Call

Ten Years Later

At the 1979 spring training, the Yankees were in Clearwater, Florida, where the Phillies also trained. I had led the World Series with the highest batting average in my Rookie year. Pete Rose was the first baseman of the Phillies in 1979. Jim "Catfish" Hunter, a Hall of Fame pitcher, was my roommate. We never waited in the hotel to get on the team bus. We either took a cab or walked to the stadium.

So, every day we arrived at the stadium very early. Pete was taking batting practice while Catfish and I walked out onto the field. Pete took his last swing and jogged around the bases. When he stepped on third, he didn't hesitate and came right to us. He stuck out his hand to say hi to Catfish.

> **I do not want to ever forget what an epic experience it was to be able to suit up with the Philadelphia Phillies as a thirteen-year-old and take batting practice and infield practice with them.**

After an exchange of words, he turned to me and in an arrogant way, stuck out his hand and said, "Pete Rose."

The Call: Can They Play Up?

I immediately replied, "Get lost, man!" then walked away and sat in the dugout.

I was the second hitter in the lineup for that game. My first at bat, I hit a single. There I was on first base with Pete Rose. After he called me a few names I will not repeat, I took my first stride off first base.

I said, "Never, ever say," then on my second stride, "to a thirteen-year-old kid," on my last stride, "to get lost when he asks for an autograph." Then, I promptly stole second base.

During this time, Catfish Hunter had the bench ready to go and help if Rose decided to punch me. He had told them I had told Pete Rose to get lost. After I got back to the dugout, Catfish asked me why I told Rose to get lost. I told him the story and he burst out laughing. The entire team then knew what and why the incident happened.

To this day, I do not think Pete Rose should be allowed into the Hall of Fame. Not because he didn't give me an autograph, but because he broke the one rule that is posted on every door of every Major League clubhouse. It is the only rule posted. It is a sacred rule. The Rule 21 topics are: Misconduct, Gift for Defeating an Opposing

Team, Gifts to Umpires, Betting on Ball Games, Violence or Misconduct in Interleague Games, Other Misconduct, and Rule to Be Posted in Every Clubhouse.

Line Drive

You are not a nice person when you do something nice. You are only a nice person when you ARE nice consistently. Pete Rose didn't care who I was, nor did he even know what I was referring to since that was ten years ago. He did hear how to be nice. Consistency is the closest thing to perfection. We will never be perfect, but we can choose to be consistent in our character.

CHAPTER 7

The Call: Knee Surgery and No Front Teeth at Sixteen Years Old

I was only fifteen years old when my knee started hurting. I did not tell anyone, not even Blake, about the pain. I would play football, basketball, and baseball with a torn ACL. A small bone would pop out and I would take my thumbs and push it back in. I did that all year. Eventually, it became worse and I would fall down, push the knee back in place, and go on playing.

Finally, I knew I needed to go to an orthopedic surgeon. Dad made the call and I traveled to Louisville, Kentucky to see Dr. Kotcamp. He was the Cleveland

The Call

Browns orthopedic surgeon. Needless to say, after the x-rays, he declared that I had torn my ACL. He wanted to know how long ago, and I told him over one year. He couldn't believe that I played all those sports activities with a torn ACL. We set an appointment for surgery on my right knee and I was back to see Dr. Kotcamp in three days. This was the very first cadaver transplant ever performed on an athlete.

A day after the surgery, the doctor came to see me. I had a cast on from the very top of my thigh to below my ankle. He told me that I could go home if I could lift my leg up off the mattress. I tried and tried while he was there, but I had no success. He reached into his doctor's long white jacket and pulled out a syringe. He picked up my leg and placed the needle right under my heel. He told me that he was going to count to three and let go of my leg and if I couldn't hold my leg up, the needle would go into my heel. He counted to three and I was straining to keep my leg up with all my might. He let go! He took the needle away and my leg slammed on the bed. The pain was terrible. The only satisfaction I had was that I vomited and got that snowy white jacket of his, not so snowy white.

I stayed up all night trying to lift my leg. The next morning Dr. Kotcamp came through the door and I was rapidly lifting my leg off and on the mattress. He saw the speed that I was doing it and said without any expression that I was being discharged that morning.

I have a very high pain tolerance, so I worked extremely hard on my rehabilitation and was playing basketball in eight weeks. I had to wear this ridiculously large knee brace. Back then they were heavy with metal side bars and hinges. I thought that I would not get a college scholarship in basketball or baseball because of that ridiculous knee brace.

No Front Teeth

Spring came and we were on our home baseball field for the fourth game of the season. As usual, we took infield practice before the game. I was playing shortstop and Coach Meadows hit me my first ground ball. I bent down to catch the ball and the ball hit a rock which made it pop up and hit me square in the mouth. I did not hit the ground. I stood there, bent over at the waist, spitting blood out of my mouth. As I was spitting blood, the front top four teeth came out root and all.

Coach Meadows quickly put my teeth in a cloth and a dad of one of my teammates took me quickly to the local dentist. Mom and Dad had not arrived yet for the game. As I got into Mr. Salmon's truck, I asked how bad it looked.

He had the soothing words, "Oh, it's terrible, your teeth must have gone through your lip because you have a huge hole. Look!"

> **What a way to soothe a sixteen-year-old boy who just lost his four front teeth!**

He turned the rear-view mirror and I saw that my mouth was five times the size it should be.

When we arrived at the dentist office, the dentist quickly took X-rays which showed that the entire upper bone structure had been cracked. He told me he could not put the teeth back into the sockets because of the break and that there was a possibility that more teeth might die and have to be pulled.

I had too many stitches in my lip and my gums to count. I looked hideous. The only thing I could eat was milk shakes. However, Coach Meadows ordered a hockey mask for me and I pitched the very next day. I had to look very intimidating with the mask on and throwing the ball in the low ninety-miles-per-hour. In fact, I thought that I would have a little fun with my new appearance. I threw the first pitch of the game just over the head of the opponents' leadoff man. The opposing team was intimidated, and I pitched a very easy game after that first pitch.

Line Drive

It is extremely difficult to explain my feelings when I was told that I tore my anterior cruciate ligament (ACL). The ACL provides 85 percent of the restraining force to anterior tibial displacement at 30 degrees and 90 degrees of knee flexion. In other words, it is an extremely important ligament not just for everyday normal life, but especially in an athlete's life. I knew that there was a possibility that I might never play a sport again.

The Call

So, I took on the statement Dad would always make when big obstacles or intense athletic moments came, "When you are wrestling a gorilla you don't stop when you get tired, you stop when the gorilla gets tired."

The same mental picture came to me when my front teeth were knocked out by a bad hop. I didn't quit. Dad's saying is very important to this day and every day.

> **Praise God, all things are possible with HIM!**

I took on the enemy with a vengeance.

Every single day I had the goal of doing more reps with the weighted boot to get my knee as strong as I could.

So, let me ask you, "What problem do you have today that could seem insurmountable? What are you willing to do to get to the other side? What is holding you back from getting into the ring with a gorilla?"

"With men this is impossible, but with God all things are possible." (NKJV)

I played against Tommy John in the World Series and he then became a New York Yankee and my roommate on the road. He has an elbow ligament surgery named after him. I could have had the ACL surgery named after me because I was the first athlete to have it. Oh well, I was only sixteen. You can look it up in the medical journal. Maybe it should be called the "Brian Doyle Surgery."

CHAPTER 8

The Call: I Know Who I Am to Marry

Connie Payton

Having free time now, I noticed, for the second time, this girl who was one year behind me in high school. She was gorgeous! She became the Basketball Sweetheart for Caverna High School, and she was only a sophomore. Her name was Connie Payton.

The Call: I Know Who I Am to Marry

1971 - I knew who I was going to marry...Connie Payton

I was love sick. I am a determined guy, an "A" type personality, someone who can and will endure. I knew this was the girl I was going to marry. A year before, when I was a sophomore and Connie was a freshman, I asked her to go to the Athletic Banquet with me. She finally accepted. I borrowed my sister's car, which was a Cadillac. I was so excited. Everything went well until we got in the car after the banquet and I had just tossed my newly acquired batting trophy in the front seat. Connie didn't see it, as it was after dark, and yes, she sat on it and broke it. I didn't care!

Later, when we did go out on a date, she didn't know which twin brother she was with because my brother-in-law loved to tease her and tell her she had gone out with Blake. Fortunately, that Monday I had mentioned Blake and she knew that I was the twin who had taken her out.

Connie was very leery of us going out together, because I had dated a girl from a rival high school. She thought that I was using her to make the other girl jealous. I did everything that I knew how to do to impress her.

I had a great chance to be with her when we were in a school play together. We had taken a break and she was sitting down off stage. I walked up to her, did a complete 360-degree spin, and kicked the hat she was wearing off her head. Great athletic move, only I kicked her in the head. NICE MOVE! Connie obviously was not impressed.

One day during school, that ex-girlfriend came to see me. She had skipped school and came to my school to talk. I saw her on the second floor of the school and grabbed her arm to get her out of there. While I was walking down the steps, guess who was coming up the steps? You guessed correctly, Connie. I knew that I was in big trouble!

I tried calling her that night, but only her mother would answer the phone and would not allow me to talk to Connie. I talked to our mutual friend, Betsy Houk. She told me what I had to do to convince Connie that I was sorry and that my love for her was sincere.

So, the next morning, I went to Connie's homeroom. I knocked on the classroom door and said that Connie Payton was wanted in the Principal's office. As soon as she came out, I quickly closed the door, picked her up, put her over my shoulder, and carried her to the Annual Room. (I had the key because I was on the committee to edit the school yearbook.) She kept saying she was going to yell, and I told her to go ahead, because it would be embarrassing if someone saw us. I got her into the Annual Room, got down on my knees, told her how sorry I was, and she was the only girl for me.

This action of mine did something to Connie, because we have not been separated since that day. I had heard the call to action, a call to humbleness, a call to love. Connie has been my rock for forty-five plus years and she is the best person that I have ever known.

I also found out that there is a price to pay when you are in love. It is not only humbling yourself, sometimes it is even more. Spring had sprung, and I was at a gas station filling up the car. A car load of guys from the rival high school jumped out of the car, grabbed me, and threw me into the back seat. They held me so that I could not move and drove me two or three miles into a very dark and secluded field with a forest surrounding it. They dragged me out of the car and threw me on the ground. There was a boy on each of my legs and arms holding me down. The fifth boy had a knife and started cutting my right pants leg all the way up to my waist. He then cut my underwear and stated that I was going to be castrated. He started cutting the inside of my thigh about an inch at a time. He wasn't going deep, just nicking the tip of the blade as he moved up.

Every one of the boys started laughing very loud. They were enjoying the show. The guy who was holding down my right leg was laughing so hard I felt him loosen the pressure. I screamed and with all my might, kicked my leg loose. When I kicked my leg loose, my knee hit the arm of the guy who had the knife and the knife went into his side. He fell back and all the guys quit holding me down to help their friend.

I got up and started running. I found the road and knew where I was. I cut across farms and homes afraid to get on the road where they could find me. I got back to my car and went home. Mom, Dad, and Blake were not there. I cleaned up and went to Connie's house. I

Act on the first, learn from the second, and seek for the answers on the third. That is fun and will help make you successful.

couldn't be alone at that time. I had to see someone and feel safe.

Line Drive

I know what you may be thinking. How can a sixteen-year-old know who he is going to marry?

How can a person explain the ways of God? I can't answer those questions, but I can say I knew that I knew Connie was the woman for me. It was not just her beauty on the outside; she had such beauty on the inside.

Have you ever gotten the feeling that you knew that you knew? If you haven't acted upon it, do it now before it is too late. There will probably be situations and circumstances to overcome. However, it is more than worth it. There are things that you know that you know. There are things that you know that you don't know. There are things that you don't know that you don't know.

CHAPTER 9

The Call: You Can't Play Football

My Right Knee Kept Me from Playing

My junior year I did not play football. Dr. Kotcamp made the call to the house and said that I could not play. Because I was not playing, Blake did not want to play. Therefore, we worked very hard during the football season on our basketball and baseball skills. We both desired to play college basketball and baseball. I also had more time to see Connie that fall of my junior year, which was a huge positive.

Our senior year in high school, Blake was being pressured into playing football again. I let him know that it would be fine with me if he played. He was the quarterback, defensive safety, punter, kickoff returner, and punt returner. I kept the stats on the sideline and felt so sorry for Blake. Every team knew if they could hurt him they had a great chance to win.

That winter I had many letters from NCAA Division I universities, contacting me about playing baseball and basketball. The pressure was off now. I knew that I was going to be able to go to college on a full scholarship. I loved both sports so much, although basketball was my favorite.

During my baseball season, our games were loaded with Major League scouts coming to see both Blake and me play. I was still wearing the big awkward knee brace. Dad came to me one day and said that I should take the knee brace off. He thought that my knee would get stronger and all the scouts would not have a question about my knee's health. He also made the call to Coach Meadows and asked if Blake and me could run the 60-yard dash for the scouts before our next game. It happened and I barely beat Blake. Because of Dad making the call, scouts did not have a doubt about my knee.

The Call: You Can't Play Football

Our Amazing High School Team

We had a very good team. Allow me to explain just how good my high school team was my senior year. First, we had three pitchers that threw in the 90 miles per hour range. Dennis Rock was 6'2" and was our third starter. Blake pitched left-handed and was our ace. Blake had never lost a game in his life. I was the number two pitcher. We also had three other pitchers, Kelly Logsdon, Charles Farrell, and Gary Larimore, who would be aces on any other high school team.

The only game we lost that year was against a huge rival at their ballpark. They pitched a left-hander against us. I hit a home run in the fourth inning and the score stayed 1-0 until the seventh. Dennis Rock was pitching and unfortunately, he walked the first batter. They sacrificed bunted and he threw the ball into right field. The runner scored. They bunted again, and Dennis did the same thing and Glasgow beat us 2-1.

The very next week we had the conference tournament. We faced Glasgow again and the same pitcher that beat us was on the bump. The third inning was so awesome. Our seventh hitter got up to the plate and hit a home run. Our eighth hitter got up and hit a home run. Our ninth hitter hit a home run. Then Blake, our lead-off hitter, got up and hit the flag waving in center field. Four back-to-back-to-back-to-back home runs. In fact, we went on to win the Kentucky State High School Baseball Championship. Our record was 36-1.

The team was amazing. We had three players who went on to play professional baseball. There were quite a few Major League scouts who stated our team was the best high school baseball team they had ever seen. The three games for the Kentucky State Championship were not even close. We won two games by five runs and one game by ten runs. We were one of the smallest high schools in Kentucky and back then there were no divisions. The final game we played a large school, Owensboro High School.

Our head coach was Coy Meadows who had played for the University of Tennessee. He had played against Denny in high school. Our assistant coach was Bruce Gentry who was from Caverna and played college baseball at Denny's alma mater, Morehead State University. We had the best coaching staff in the state of Kentucky. Put these two wonderful coaches with eight or nine very good athletes and you will do something special.

1972 - Caverna High 1972 Kentucky State HS Baseball Champions

Props to Wayne Bowsher, Kelly Logsdon, Gary Larimore, Charles Farrell, Glenn Martin, Dennis Rock, Tommy Renick, Leonard Tribble, Mark Davis, J.T. Neely, Robbie Williams, Joey Brown, Tommy Bale, Phillip Cobb, Ronnie Woodard, Dennis Brown, and of course Blake Doyle. Guys, you were a great team.

Easy to see how great when our earned run average at the end of the year was 1.02 and our opponents gave up 7.70 runs.

Line Drive

Once again, I had a trial in my life. James 1:2-4 comes to life, "Consider it pure joy, my brothers and sisters, whenever you face trials of many kinds, because you know that the testing of your faith produces perseverance. Let perseverance finish its work so that you may be mature and complete, not lacking anything." It does not say "if" you face trials; it says "whenever" you face trials. We are not exempt from facing trials. This was just the beginning of all the trials that I was to face in my life. That is why I am writing this book.

Kentucky State High School Baseball Championship

Stay with me through the entire book and see the hope and grace of God.

Caverna was one of the smallest schools, if not the smallest school in the state of Kentucky. There were no divisions in high school athletics at the time. The smallest school would often have to play the largest school. In 1961, Caverna made it to the Kentucky High School Baseball

The Call: You Can't Play Football

State Tournament. A team had to win three games to win the single elimination championship. What is unheard of today in baseball is to have a pitcher pitch two games in three days.

My brother, Denny pitched the first game on a Thursday where he struck out fifteen batters. He played shortstop the second game on Friday. He pitched the championship game on Saturday and struck out fifteen batters. He held the record of thirty strikeouts in the State Tournament competition and won.

1961 - Blake and me looking up at big brother after his High School State Championship, and we still do!

The Call

Eleven years later in 1972, Caverna was again in the Kentucky High School Baseball State Tournament. Thursday, I pitched the first game of the State Tournament and struck out fifteen batters. Friday, the second game, I played shortstop and Dennis Rock, who eventually played for the Kansas City Royals minor league, pitched the second game. Saturday, Blake was to pitch the championship game, but he hurt his back in the second game, making a wonderful diving play as our second baseman. He could still play second base right-handed, but his back was too sore to pitch left-handed. Yes, Blake is ambidextrous.

I got the call from Coach Meadows, asking if I could pitch the final game. Of course, I said yes. I pitched the third game and struck out sixteen batters. I broke my brother's record and as far as I know, it still stands as the record today.

Little Caverna High School has won two State Championships. Each son of the Doyle family was involved. Our little towns of Cave City and Horse Cave were so excited afterwards. We had parades and ceremonies for three days. It was awesome to be State Champions.

The Call: You Can't Play Football

The Caverna High School was made up of two towns, Cave City, where I was raised, and Horse Cave, where my future wife, Connie, was raised. Caverna was an independent high school and was the first integrated high school in the state of Kentucky.

Out of these two little towns came Charlie Moran, a catcher in the early 1900s who played for the St. Louis Cardinals and later became a Major League umpire. Then there was Clarence Wilson, who became a Harlem Globetrotter and was one of my youth league coaches. As a junior high student, I practiced basketball with a senior, Clarence Glover, who played for the Boston Celtics.

> **I do not think there is another small area in the US with less than 2,000 residents that has had that many men play professionally.**

Joe Campbell, who was in Denny's class, played in the Major Leagues with the Chicago Cubs. Denny played in the Major Leagues for the Phillies, Angels, and Red Sox. Dennis Rock, who played on my Caverna State Championship Team, played for the Kansas City

Royals minor league. Of course, Blake played for the Orioles and Reds for three years in AAA baseball and made it to the Major Leagues as the Colorado Rockies Hitting Coach. I played in the Major Leagues for the Yankees and A's. It is amazing that Cave City and Horse Cave had eight men who played in professional baseball and basketball.

Line Drive

Have you ever been the little person that had to go up against the much larger person? Have you had a problem that you thought was so big that there was no way to get out of it?

> *Do you have a giant to go up against? God is bigger!*

I believe that one must look at oneself in these situations. One must look back at the times that God intervened and by His grace, mercy, and power, solved that huge problem. By looking at past victories, one can go into the present and face that huge problem with great confidence. It is not how big you are or how big your problem, it is always how big your God is. How big is He?

The Call: You Can't Play Football

In the Bible, David knew how big his God was when he took on and defeated Goliath. Go and read that story in 1 Samuel 17. He knew that God was big enough to defeat a giant.

CHAPTER 10

The Call: Texas Rangers

The 1972 Major League Amateur Draft

Right before the second game of the State Championship, Dad got the call. The Texas Rangers had picked me as the seventy-sixth pick in the fourth round of the 1972 Major League Draft. Blake was drafted by the Baltimore Orioles in the fourth round as the ninety-sixth pick. We were drafted in the first one hundred picks in the nation. Now decisions had to be made. Were we going to college or sign to play professional baseball? My focus was winning the Kentucky State Championship. The last time Caverna High School won a state championship was when my older brother, Denny, was a senior at Caverna.

The Call: Texas Rangers

We decided to sign professional contracts, which paid for one of the greatest days of my life. We had a black and white Philco television. Mom and Dad had only seen a color TV a few times. After Blake and I got our signing bonus, we went to the Devore Furniture Shop. Mom worked next door at Parkland Drugs. We wanted to buy a color TV. So, we had Mom walk next door and she picked out the TV. Denny was going to be on TV Saturday. It was called the Saturday Game of the Week. It was the only Major League Baseball game that ran on TV. We had the TV delivered mid-morning on game day.

We knew that Dad always went to the high school on Saturday morning just to check to see everything was running properly throughout the school. When he pulled up in the driveway, Blake and I quickly ran out the back door and grabbed Dad to blindfold him. He was not very happy about it. We brought him inside and sat him in "his" chair. When the music started for the Game of the Week, we took the blindfold off. Dad was able to watch his oldest son play in color. It was an epic day.

In mid-June, I was off to Geneva, New York, to play with the rookie ball team for the Texas Rangers. It was extremely hard to leave Connie behind, but I had to because I was following my dream to play Major League Baseball. I walked into the clubhouse and the first thing that I saw was a cigarette machine and a tub of ice and beer. I had never seen beer in my whole life! What is this? Professional baseball is like this?

My locker room in high school was ten times nicer than this one. I was given a uniform and told to report onto the field as soon as possible. When I got on the field I was in shock. All these college players were huge and very intimidating. The only thing I could do was act like I belonged there. It was nerve wracking.

There was this little old man standing there, using a fungo bat as a prop, he said, "You, Brian Doyle, get out there at shortstop and take some ground balls."

As soon as I got on the field and caught the first three grounders, I was perfectly at home. However, after getting off the field, I was very uncomfortable. I lived in a home with four other guys, all from college. I was the youngest and smallest guy on the team. I felt more than awkward when off the field. I had no social skills. I am serious, NO social skills. All that I had ever done was play sports. Talk about a person being dysfunctional; that was me. Baseball had become the only entity where I felt comfortable.

The very first day, the manager of the team said that he was not to be called Coach, or Mr., or any other name except Sarge. He was a very large man with a husky voice. He would scare you to death if you had a face-to-face talk with him. There were two other shortstops on the team, both from college, and I played every game. Being the youngest guy on the team, I could not and would not, go with them to the bars. It quickly became clear to me that if I took care of my body, not go out and party, that I had a better chance than they did to get to the Major Leagues.

My first professional baseball game was one to remember. It was written in the *New York Times*. Here is a part of the article.

GENEVA, N.Y., June 24—The first woman umpire in organized baseball, Mrs. Bernice Gera, resigned in tears tonight after having worked her first game.

The 41-year-old umpire from Jackson Heights, Queens, ejected Nolan Campbell, manager of the Auburn

The Call

Phillies, after a disputed play at second base in the fourth inning of the Geneva Rangers' 4-1 victory in the opener of the New York-Penn League season.

"The argument had nothing to do with it," Mrs. Gera explained. "I had my bags packed before the game. I just wanted to prove a point. The only thing I've learned from baseball is how to be bitter."

Mrs. Gera received a contract after the State Court of Appeals affirmed last Jan. 19 the judgments of the State Human Rights Division and lower courts that she had been denied an umpire's job in the minors because of her sex.

The play that was disputed was one in which I was involved. There were two outs with a runner on first base. A ground ball was hit to our second baseman, he flipped me the ball, and I stepped on second base for the force out. Mrs. Gera yelled safe as she spread her arms for the sign.

I said, "Safe?"

She quickly said that I did not tag the runner.

I said, "This is a force out, I don't have to tag the runner."

She quickly said, "Oh, you are right" and yelled "Out!"

Then came the Phillies manager, Nolan Campbell, out of the dugout to argue. She threw him out of the game. It was hilarious to watch.

It was in the fourth or fifth game that I struck out. I made the call to my Dad because it was the first time that I had ever experienced a strike out. I told him that I didn't know if I could be good enough to play professional baseball. He encouraged me and told me that the guys I was facing were very good pitchers and everyone strikes out. That phone call did not make me feel better, but it did keep me from coming home.

My first year in professional baseball was extremely hard! I had never been by myself. I was with a bunch of college guys. Plus, I felt like I was just another player, not a teammate. I quickly learned that professional baseball was not about team play. It was every player for himself. That was something that I had never experienced. Everything was team first. That was how I was raised. I was absolutely heart broken. The game of baseball had completely changed. No one wanted to help their teammate. In fact, everyone was for himself.

I came home a couple of days early so that I could enroll at Western Kentucky University. The last day of the season the fans voted me the most popular player. I received a set of luggage in the mail. That made me feel so much better. I still had the problem of being alone. It was so hard for me to go to professional baseball after being with a twin brother all the time.

In 1973, I went to the Texas Ranger A club in Gastonia, North Carolina. I had the same feelings that I had the year before. I was the smallest and youngest on the team again. I kept to myself and kept very quiet. It was a horrific year psychologically. On an off day, I flew home for just one day to see Connie. After that small trip, which I couldn't afford, the very next day I went to a jewelry store and bought an engagement ring. I knew that I could not play baseball another year with that much loneliness . So, when the season was over, as soon as I got home to Cave City, I asked Connie to be my wife. Surprisingly she said yes. So, at nineteen years old, I got married. Connie was barely eighteen years old. We were kids getting married. Not a smart move, but we made it.

We got married on December 21, 1973, in Horse Cave Baptist Church. Despite our youth, I did love her very much. She was the girl of my dreams. I felt so fortunate that I married the most beautiful girl in the world.

1973 - Wedding Day! Friday, December 21

That evening we had a huge snow storm. We very carefully drove to Louisville, Kentucky for our honeymoon. We stayed at the Executive Inn Airport Hotel Saturday and Sunday. After that we lived with Connie's mother through January. Connie's father had died when she was fourteen years old. We then moved to Mom and Dad Doyle's house during February 1974. Then it was off to Plant City, Florida, for Spring Training.

Sir Sherlock of Cambridge

During our first month of marriage, I spent most of my time with my sister Janice and twin brother Blake playing golf. The second month of marriage, we bought our first pet, an Irish Setter puppy, "Sir Casey Sherlock of Cambridge." A puppy in the Jake and Virginia Doyle household was a set up for stress. Especially when Mom found out that Connie had given a bath to Sherlock in her bathtub.

When we left for Spring Training and got to Plant City, Florida with Sherlock, it was difficult to find a place to live that allowed pets. We rented a proverbial SHACK! It was horrible! Spring Training was six weeks long and we couldn't wait to get out of there.

Our first assignment as a married couple was Pittsfield, Massachusetts with the Texas Rangers AA team. We arrived in town and had the same housing difficulty with a very active young Sherlock. We finally found a farmer to take our dog. Our Sherlock had a good home with plenty of land to run and play. Now, we were able to rent a home for the season in a place where they didn't understand our Kentucky accent and thought the Texas Rangers were law enforcement officers coming to town. We are forever thankful for Don and Marcia Clark taking us under their wing that year. Minor League Booster Clubs are invaluable to young players!

Our team was good. Eventually, we had eleven players reach the Major Leagues. I was only twenty years old and again the youngest player on the team. The season ended in Pittsfield and we moved back to Kentucky for the off-season. We rented an upstairs apartment in Bowling Green, Kentucky. Connie was now pregnant and working at a lady's department store named Norman's. I found a job at Sears, working in the Men's Clothing Department. Connie did not go to Spring Training in 1975 but stayed with her Mom so that she could see her doctor. So, I headed to Plant City by myself.

Line Drive

WOW! It is extremely difficult to go through life not having an identity of your own. Being a twin, I was still trying to have an identity of my own. I was used to being called a "Doyle twin." I was still not comfortable in being called Brian. I thought Connie was the answer. I was still just a twenty-year-old kid. I had no idea how to be a loving husband. It was so hard for me. I did not know how to feel, act, or respond to situations. By no means was I the knight on the white steed rescuing Connie. By no means was I her romantic hero. I didn't think that I was good enough for the very first time in my life. I was extremely sad. I thank God that He loves me. I wasn't saved, but I know now that He was pursuing me.

Do you know that God is a pursuing God? He is pursuing you if you do not know Him as Lord and Savior. God had given me a beautiful girl to ask to marry me. I wouldn't be alone anymore. I pursued her relentlessly. Ladies love to be pursued. I really thought that was the answer to success. I loved her

> **If I had only known that before we got married.**

very much, but I was relying on our marriage to make me successful.

> *"This book of the law shall not depart from your mouth, but you shall meditate on it day and night, and be careful to do everything that is written in it. Then you will make your ways prosperous and then you will have success." (Joshua 1:8)*

CHAPTER 11

The Call: I'm Going to Be a Father

I was playing in Lynchburg, Virginia, with the Texas Ranger A team. Connie got the call that she needed to see the doctor. It was 1975 and I was trying to make a name for myself as a hitter. I had asked the Ranger's Minor League Director to place me down to A ball so that I could play every day. I knew that I should be much better than I was. I needed to play to get better. However, I was constantly thinking about Connie's and the baby's health.

There are many people that think playing professional baseball is such a glamorous profession. I can tell you it is an extremely sacrificing profession. You are away from family half the time. Personally, I had to negotiate my

The Call: I'm Going to Be a Father

contract every year. In the Minor Leagues you get paid for the months that you play. I had to try and find a job in the off-season. Sometimes that meant 4 to 5 part-time jobs. It was rare to get a full-time job because the prospective employer knew I was leaving in late February for Spring Training.

The Baby Call

I got the call from Connie's mother that she was going into labor. I asked permission to leave the club and fly back to Kentucky to be with Connie. I got home and went directly to the hospital. Connie was having regular labor pains, but her body would not dilate to have the baby. They kept pumping her with medication to promote labor and also pain medication. She went through this for eighteen hours! Our son, Kirk, was finally born. He literally busted through. What should have happened was a "C Section." It was a very difficult delivery. Back then, the expectant father was not allowed back in the room with his wife. I stayed in the "Father's Waiting Room" all that time. When the nurse came out to tell me that I had a son, I was excited and numb. I didn't know how to act because my adrenaline was so up and down. I was alone in the waiting room and all I could think of was the Bible story of Abraham and Isaac. I just had a son! Could I love God enough to sacrifice my newborn to God? It was then that I remembered that God did show openly His love by sacrificing His Son. It was then that I started thinking on spiritual things.

I had to go back to Lynchburg to play. The job of being a professional baseball player is not only not glamorous, it is pressure! Would I be able to make enough money in the off-season to support Connie and Kirk? When would I be able to hold my son? I was there so long for the delivery that I was told that I needed to get back as soon as Connie delivered. Having a baby is one of the most bonding, loving times a husband and wife can have, and I missed out. It did not happen. It was, "Great, I'm a Dad, see you when I can."

Before I flew out to Kentucky for the birth of our son, I held a team meeting and told them that Connie and I were stuck on two names: Brandon or Kirk. So, I asked them to vote on the name and the name with the most votes would be his name. Kirk won out almost unanimously. We were thrilled to learn later in life, Kirk means "Dweller of the Church."

Connie and six-week-old Kirk arrived in Lynchburg, Virginia to "visit" for just a week. I did an unthinkable thing! I saw Kirk and wanted to hold him. He was asleep, and I woke him up. I didn't know anything about that! It was time for him to see his father.

> **Even though the intimacy was missing in naming our first born, God had a plan.**

Fortunately, our new lifelong friends, Terry and Barbara Falwell, found an apartment for us to stay the rest of the season and also for the off-season. We finally did it! We lived in one place, Lynchburg, for the entire baseball season and off-season. That was the longest we had lived in one spot since we had been married and it helped us grow as a family. Thank you, Terry and Barbara. That time in Lynchburg was paramount to our future married life!

I had several jobs that the Falwell family found for me. I built truck bodies for the Falwell Company. I also worked as a referee for football and basketball, and opened the town's basketball gym, overseeing it each weekend.

I did leave Connie and Kirk for a week. Denny was in the 1975 Playoffs and the World Series with the Boston Red Sox. Denny flew me to Boston to be a part of his lifetime dream. There were many rainouts during the playoff series, so it seemed a very long time to be separated. However, when Denny's team made it to the World Series that year, he flew Connie, Kirk, and the whole family up to watch. What a memory! Kirk's first time at a Major League game. A World Series in Boston!

Line Drive

Twenty-one years old and a father. In the father's waiting room, God reminded me of Abraham and Isaac. I had just had a son, could I love someone enough to kill my son for that person? Just the thought of that was mind blowing. I knew that it was true that Abraham was obedient, however, God stopped him and gave him a ram that was caught in a thicket for him to sacrifice. That was the first time in a long time that I thought of God not stopping the death of His own Son. I did not think much after that about spiritual things, because I was thinking about going back to play baseball and the pressure of leaving my wife and son.

God is always giving man circumstances and situations to call them to Himself. He is knocking at our heart's door. We easily get distracted and ignore His knocking. I did and how I wish I had not. Are you feeling that knocking at your door? Please, I beg you not to ignore Him.

The Call: Learn How to Hit or Be Released

In the Spring of 1976, the Bicentennial year of our nation, once again we were off to Spring Training. This time it was much easier to find a duplex to live with our baby, rather than an Irish Setter! That spring was extremely tough for me. I had gone to Spring Training with the mindset that I was going to learn how to hit to the opposite field. I was labeled as a hitter who could only pull the ball. I knew if I was not successful at hitting the ball to the opposite field that I would be released. Unfortunately, I got one hit the whole of Spring Training and that was a little blooper over the short-stop's head. At least it was to the opposite field. I knew I was going to be released by the end of Spring Training.

The staff had their meeting about who was going to be released. A former A Ball coach, Rich Donnelly, stood up for me and said not to release me as I should be on a team just to show the other players a model for a great work ethic. It was Rich who kept me from getting released. I was put on the AA roster as a utility infielder.

Our next stop was San Antonio, Texas. We arrived, found a nice apartment, unpacked, settled in, and in a very short period of time I was sent to AAA Sacramento, California. The very first game in San Antonio, our third baseman broke his thumb tagging someone out in the first inning. I took his place playing third base. The light bulb came on! My first at bat, I hit a double to left center (opposite field). My second at bat, I hit a home-run to right field. My third at bat, I hit a single to the opposite field. My fourth at bat, I hit another double to the opposite field.

I had learned how to hit to the opposite field! I stayed in San Antonio for only three weeks and was

The Call: I'm Going to Be a Father

promoted to Sacramento AAA Ball. Guess who was the AAA Manager? Rich Donnelly! Connie and Kirk were left in San Antonio! Connie started packing and called her Mom to ask if she would fly to Texas and drive with her to California. Mrs. Payton, at sixty-three, made her first ever flight with Connie's niece, Melaine, as a travel companion.

They all set out driving to California. They stopped in El Paso, Texas for a few days because Connie had driven so long with hard contacts in her eyes that she had cut her eyes. There in El Paso they went to an emergency room, Connie's eyes were patched, and they went to a hotel to rest for a few days. The things baseball wives do for their husbands!

Once Connie and Kirk were in Sacramento with me I became extremely comfortable with myself as a player. I was the leadoff hitter for the team. I played third base every day. The combination of San Antonio and Sacramento season, I hit over .300. I knew that the next year I was going to go to Major League Spring Training and compete for the starting second baseman job. I had learned how to hit to the opposite field with authority. Things were really looking up.

Line Drive

It is not easy to change. Most people look at change as a negative. I had to change in my hitting style or I was going to be released, never to play professional baseball again. I had to change, and the change had to be drastic. I only had one hit the entire Spring Training! This is the life lesson that I had learned.

When a person is seen giving his or her all to improve, someone is always watching the effort. Rich Donnelly was watching. Thank You, God! When the "bell rang" and I had to perform, I was successful. I was a less than average hitter, but by the time the season ended I was in AAA hitting over .300 in batting average. There was lots of talk that I was going to be the Texas Ranger's starting second baseman in the Major Leagues the next year.

> **Sometimes one has to fail miserably to learn how to succeed.**

The Call: I'm Going to Be a Father

What do you have to drastically change? Through failure comes success, so don't be afraid, don't care how you look, don't care what people think. You are changing to get better. The end result should be to care what God thinks.

CHAPTER 12

The Call: Traded to the Yankees

Connie and I went back to Kentucky and rented an upstairs apartment from a sweet elderly lady, Mrs. Reynolds. This was a wonderful off-season, full of a little boy's energy, snow, and family. A nice respite after the 1976 season! The upstairs apartment was a 10-minute walk to my Mom and Dad's where I grew up.

I drove thirty minutes to Bowling Green, Kentucky to find some type of work. I went to the mall there and walked into a high-end men's clothing store. They had the nicest clothing in a sixty-mile radius. I met with the manager of Golden Farley and he offered me a job. It was for little money an hour, but the commission was 6 percent. I accepted the job and drove back to see Connie and tell her the good news. This was on Friday and I was going to start work the following Monday.

Now, Blake had come home that Friday evening and went to Bowling Green to find a job for himself on Saturday, which I did not know. He came home that Saturday night and came to our apartment. He was excited about getting a job at Golden Farley in Bowling Green. He said that he walked in and the manager came directly to him and shook his hand and stated that he was all excited about him coming to work on Monday.

> **Sometimes being a twin is challenging!**

I stood up and said, "You took my job!"

I explained to him that I had gotten the job on Friday and the manager thought that Blake was me. I told Blake that we were going to walk into Golden Farley on Monday morning and get everything straightened out. When we got there and walked into the manager's office he was astonished. He couldn't utter a word. I spoke first. I explained the situation and said that the only thing he could do was to hire us both. He did.

The Call

One afternoon at work I got "The Call."

I answered the store phone and said, "Golden Farley, Brian Doyle, how may I assist you?"

The man answered, "This is Cedric Tallis of the New York Yankees, congratulations, you have just been traded to the Yankees."

I was speechless, mystified, saddened, and stunned all at the same time. I was really sad because I knew I had a great shot at becoming the Texas Rangers second baseman that year. I had hit .315 that summer in AA and AAA. Now, being with the Yankees, I knew that I would not get a shot at being in the Major Leagues.

Mr. Tallis said, "You made $1,000.00 a month last year, we will be putting you on the AAA roster, what do you expect to make this year?"

Still stunned I thought and said $2,000.00.

He immediately said, "Okay."

Wow, I was happy! Then I said to myself, "Tallis didn't even hesitate. I should have asked for $3,000.00." Now I was mad at myself thinking that I was such a good negotiator by doubling my salary. In addition, everybody knew that if you were in the Minor Leagues with the Yankees, it was a dead-in career ending situation. The majority owner, George Steinbrenner, would go and get players with Major League experience rather than bring up players from their Minor Leagues.

So, in March, off to Hollywood, Florida we would go. We found a small apartment to rent that was close to the Minor League Yankee complex in Hollywood. The Yankee Major League Team trained in Ft. Lauderdale a few miles north. The Yankee AAA team was located in Syracuse, New York.

One of the bright spots of that season was that Blake was in Rochester, New York with the Orioles AAA team. We were able to play against each other for the very first time. It was always a blast to be with him on the field. One of the series that we played in Syracuse, Blake and I exchanged uniforms and took batting practice and pre-game infield. No one knew the difference; no one even noticed. Both of us played second base and we both had a blast in the opposite clubhouse. At least my first year with the Yankee organization was fun because Blake and I were in the same league.

The Call

After the season, we traveled back to Kentucky. I went back to work for Golden Farley. I had arrived back in Cave City before Blake did and went to the store to see if I was to be hired back. The manager said of course. He said it in an excited tone. So, I said that Blake and I would work there if he would double our commission. He looked at me like I was crazy asking for that much. After stating a few facts reminding him of our success each month we worked there last year, he decided on a 75 percent raise on commission. I would have taken 50 percent. Blake got back a couple of days later and when I told him I had gotten him a very significant raise, he was elated.

> *Decisions need to be prayed about.*

Line Drive

Have you ever been in a situation where you had to make a decision that very moment? I learned a very important lesson the day the Yankees called my place of work.

The Call: Traded to the Yankees

They don't have to be made right at that second. If I had said that I would get back to him about my salary, I would have had time to seek good counsel. Another thing that I learned is that I should not make individual, personal decisions without talking to my wife. No decision should be made unless it is good for us.

CHAPTER 13

The Call: To Repentance!

I want to now go back to my first Spring Training with the Yankees in Hollywood, Florida. I was still disappointed that I got traded. It was like I was just going through the motions. We had rented a small apartment in Hollywood, Florida. I would come home after the day and Connie would tell me who she had met. She was going through the same thing that I was going through, feeling empty, unfulfilled, and lost. She was seeking answers and allowing Jehovah Witnesses, Mormons, and people from other religions in the apartment in hopes of finding a way to peace and joy. There had to be more to life than we were experiencing. There was a big hole in our lives that needed to be filled.

The Call: To Repentance!

We were with a new organization and did not know anyone. As usual, I got to the clubhouse very early. I knew I would be the first person there. When I walked in I was shocked. There stood a player already there.

He walked up to me, stuck out his hand and said, "Hi, I'm Marv Thompson."

During this time in my life, I was an arrogant young man who was also very crass, and I said, "You have only one tit."

He quickly stated that I was very observant. He was born with no pectoral muscle on the right side. He turned and went back to the business of getting on his uniform. After I got dressed, I went to him and introduced myself. Marv turned out to be a very nice guy. He made sure that I felt welcomed in the Yankee organization. He would introduce me to the players and coaches. He went out of his way to be nice to me. No one in professional baseball had ever done that.

Connie met Karen, Marv's wife. She saw that Connie was letting people of all kinds of faiths come into the apartment and talk with her. Connie found out that Karen was a Christian. One Sunday she took Connie to the Coral

Ridge Presbyterian Church of Ft. Lauderdale where the pastor there was known as a good preacher. He was even on TV. His name was Dr. D. James Kennedy. That Easter Sunday Connie, little Kirk, and I went to that church. I was impressed with his preaching.

Spring Training ended, and we were off to Syracuse, New York. We drove north in a baseball players' caravan. The caravan consisted of the Thompsons, the DeRosas, Dave Rajisich, and Dennis Werth. We were driving a new green van that had a refrigerator and a large sleeping space in the back. Driving on the Pennsylvania Turnpike, we were side-swiped by an eighteen-wheeler. This happened at night with Connie and Kirk asleep in the back. Thanks to the truck driver's expertise, he laid the truck down in the median ditch. We were thankful to be alive. I had three broken ribs which I taped up tight all summer with nobody knowing. To this day, Connie never sleeps in a car while being a passenger.

Connie found a two-bedroom apartment so that two-year-old Kirk could have his own room. That didn't last very long because Karen and Marv could not find an apartment. We told them that they could stay with us until they found an apartment. Every morning Connie and I could hear them pray and read the Bible together in their bedroom. Before they went to bed they did the very same thing. Neither Marv nor Karen spoke to us about Jesus. They didn't have to; they lived out their Christianity. They stayed with us almost the entire summer.

It was a long summer because I was playing in such great pain. I would go into the restroom of the clubhouse and tape myself from the sternum to the navel every day. I learned how to play with pain. Needless to say, I was not having a good offensive year.

It was August 17 when we landed in Tidewater, Virginia. We had a four-day series there. Marv was my roommate on the road. We arrived at the hotel and each of us tried to get some rest before we were to get on the team bus. I laid on my bed and my heart was beating a hundred miles an hour. I knew, by watching Marv and Karen, that I needed Jesus in my life.

I rolled off the bed to my knees and said out loud, "God, I have made a mess of my life. I need a boss. I need you, Jesus, to be the Lord of my life. Please forgive me of my sin and fill me with Yourself."

Marv was stunned. He came over and gave me a hug. I was so excited! I felt so clean and so filled. I knew that God had a purpose for my life. I couldn't wait to tell Connie what I had done. I grabbed the hotel room phone and made the call to Connie who was back in Syracuse, New York. She answered the phone and I could tell that she was crying. I asked her what was wrong. She said nothing was wrong. She had just got off her knees to answer the phone. Connie told me that she had just prayed for Jesus to be her Lord and Savior. She accepted Jesus at the very same time that I had. Now that is our God. Born again, August 17, 1977, at the very same time. We began growing together with Marv and Karen answering our questions.

> *God's timing is perfect.*

Line Drive

There comes a time in every person's life when they ask questions like, "Why am I here? Why was I born? What is the purpose for my life? What is going to happen to me when I die?" Everyone has some type of question like those. Connie and I were personally looking for an answer. The Bible says that God loves a seeker. Well, praise God that He saved us at the very same time while we were in different states. We both got "THE CALL" to be saved and I gave a call to Connie which proves there is a God.

CHAPTER 14

Connie Made the Call: Let's Play One More Year

Being traded to the Yankees was not a real good thing because everyone knew that those in the Yankee Minor League System died there. I was more than frustrated, Connie could see that, but she wouldn't let me give up.

We talked, and she said, "Let's give it one more year."

I was somewhat shocked. She was telling me that she could go through all the work, the troubles, the travel while being a mother of a two-and-a-half-year-old boy. I agreed that we would give it a go for one more year. Then after that it was time for me to get a "real job," which Connie's grandmother kept stating that I needed to do.

Connie Made the Call: Let's Play One More Year

We were growing in our faith. We were following Jesus. Connie heeded the prompting from the Holy Spirit, so once again we were headed to Hollywood, Florida for Spring Training. Knowing this was going to be my last chance to get to the Major Leagues, I came into Spring Training in tip-top shape. I was going to show that I belonged in the Big Leagues.

Ten days before the end of Spring Training, two men walked up to me as I was leaving the clubhouse. The men were Al Rosen, the new Yankee General Manager, and George Steinbrenner. Mr. Rosen said that I was going to be picked up in a few minutes and that I was playing for the New York Yankees in Miami against the Baltimore Orioles. I was shocked! I could not wait to get to Miami. It was a little uncomfortable getting on the team bus though. I knew no one. I said hello to Thurman Munson, Reggie Jackson, Bucky Dent, and Roy White before I sat down. Just being there was exciting.

We got off the bus and the Yankee Manager, Billy Martin, told me that I would be starting and playing all nine innings. A future Hall of Famer was going to be starting his last game in Spring Training. The pitcher's name was Jim Palmer. I got even more excited. I couldn't wait for the game to begin.

I got three hits off Palmer. Then I came up to bat and the Orioles brought in a left-handed pitcher to pitch to me and I got another hit. Then the Orioles brought in another left-handed pitcher. We had a man on first base and a man on third base with one out in the top of the ninth and the score was tied. The first pitch came, and I dragged bunted the ball toward the second baseman. The man on third scored, the man on first went to second, and I beat out the bunt. I was doing my job by not hitting into a double play. After the game, Al Rosen said that I was a heads-up player.

Billy Martin came up to me and said, "Not bad going 5 for 5, old man."

I said, "Who are you calling old?"

He said he had looked me up and saw I was in AAA for three years, so I had to be old. I told him to get a roster because I was only twenty-three years old. He laughed, and I said that I was serious. I was so happy getting five hits and three of them off Jim Palmer.

I quickly remembered that Connie had made the call to play one more year. Now I was not just a number. The New York Yankees saw what I could do as a player.

Our AAA team opened the season in Phoenix, Arizona and then we had a series in Tucson, Arizona. Connie drove with little Kirk from Ft. Lauderdale, Florida and met us in Arizona. All the wives were able to see our first games. Then the wives caravanned to Tacoma, Washington. The team flew to Tacoma for opening day. I was very disappointed when I saw that I was not in the lineup. Our manager, Mike Ferraro, came to me as I was walking out of the clubhouse. He told me that I was wanted in the front office.

Why in the world would I be wanted in the front office? Had something happened to Connie? Was our son, Kirk all right?

When I walked in someone said I had "The Call." I picked up the phone and it was Al Rosen saying that I needed to get on the next plane to Baltimore, because I was going to the Big Leagues. I was so excited.

The Call

The very next thing that I did was to call Dad and let him know that I was being called up to the Major Leagues. He was very excited, but I could also hear concern in his voice. He told me that Uncle Eddie had just died. Because of that he and Mom could not come to my debut. I definitely understood.

Meanwhile, Connie had driven all the way from Ft. Lauderdale, Florida to Tacoma, Washington in a baseball wives' caravan. This caravan consisted of Karen Thompson, Paula DeRosa and her "Cisco Cat," and Connie with her "little buddy," Kirk. She had arrived in Tacoma a few hours earlier. Walking out of the office, I saw her in almost a full run from the parking lot pushing the stroller.

She was yelling out, "I found a place to live," while I was shouting, "I am going to the Big Leagues."

She was so excited. I went up to her, gave her a kiss, and told her that I was leaving immediately for Baltimore. No one was able to see my first Major League game. I wasn't disappointed, though. Every one of the family was busy, not just because Uncle Eddie died, but because everyone was helping care for my sister, Janice, too. My only sister and oldest sibling had been diagnosed with MS a few months before Connie and I were married in 1973. She had progressed to the point she needed Mom and Dad's loving constant care.

1973 - Janice "Sissy", the best athlete in the family

Line Drive

It is always amazing how God uses a woman to truly be our help mate. God gave women such intuition in so many things. Every time in my life that I had to make a decision and Connie said that she didn't feel good about it, but I did it anyway, I got into trouble. Yes, Connie was right. We men better listen to our godly wives.

The Call

*It took me a long time to figure out that every decision is not made unless it is good for **us**. When it is good for us, then I am not selfish in any way. Think about it. Oh, don't get me wrong, there were certainly times I was right, and she had to listen to me and trust the Jesus that is in me. Now, there were times when she couldn't trust me, but that's her story to tell.*

CHAPTER 15

The Call: "Doyle Second Base"

I have a thing about my fielder's glove. No one is to touch it. I always said that there were two things that cannot be touched by anyone, my wife and my glove. When I was in the dugout my glove sat next to me on my left side. There was no exception to this. The players on the Yankees noticed this and asked why I always had my glove with me and that it sat beside me. I told them why.

One occasion that is pretty funny now, was the time I was put in the game in the fifth inning. As soon as Billy Martin said, "Doyle, second base," I got up and started stretching my legs and body on the steps of the dugout while we were hitting in the bottom of the fourth inning.

The Call

As soon as the bottom half of the fourth inning ended, I grabbed my glove and went out to second base.

I went to put my glove on and I could not get a finger, not one, into my glove. The players had chewed bubble gum and took the trainer's spray freeze and stuffed my glove, frozen, to the point that there was no way to wear it. I looked into the dugout and saw everyone laughing. I played the top of the fifth inning with my hand on the outside of my glove with only the top strap of the glove, where you put your hand in the glove, holding my glove onto my hand. I had two ground balls hit to me and I made the plays. Each time I made the play, the players on the bench and the players in the field were laughing.

The very next day in Baltimore we had a rain delay. During the delay, Jim Spencer grabbed my glove quickly, threw it in a mud puddle, and stepped on it. I was furious, but I was the rookie that just got there. I picked up my glove and said nothing.

After Baltimore, we flew back to New York. We landed in LaGuardia and were waiting for our luggage when Jim Spencer, our backup first baseman, came up from behind

The Call: "Doyle Second Base"

and hit me with an airline pillow telling me welcome to New York. I had a crick in my neck for three days.

After Spencer put my glove in a mud puddle and gave me a crick in the neck, I knew I was going to craft a payback. I also found out that it was Paul Linblad, a left-handed pitcher, who had thought of the bubble gum freezing of my glove. The initiation of the rookie had officially started.

We were now back in New York and I was super excited to be playing in Yankee Stadium. I got to the ballpark with a couple of other players who were also living in the Sheraton at Hasbrouck Heights, New Jersey. I got dressed quickly and went out to the field. I went to every position spot and remembered the greats who played there. It was an awesome feeling knowing that I was going to play on that exact spot. I went back into the clubhouse, sat down in my corner locker, and got the call while in the Yankee Clubhouse for the first time.

Our trainer, Gene Monahan, came to my locker and said that I had a phone call. I thought it was Denny or Blake calling to congratulate me.

I picked up the phone and said, "Hello."

The Call

It was the owner of the Yankees, George Steinbrenner, The Boss.

He said, "Doyle, this is Steinbrenner. I am the one who got you up here and want you to go out there and bust your ass and I mean bust your ass, and don't disappoint me."

He hung up. The only word I said was hello! Wow, welcome to the Major Leagues. No pressure, right? It was kind of hilarious, but very disconcerting. Praise God I had a good game. I was raised well on how to handle authority and he had every right to do what he did. That was "The Boss."

The Yankees kept me up for at least two months. Connie kept busy with our son as she lived next door to the Thompsons and DeRosas in an apartment complex. This year the Thompsons were discipling the DeRosas. Connie felt like a single mother and for that time she was. Karen Thompson would keep Kirk sometimes so that Connie could go out selling Avon.

In the middle of the summer, Mr. Steinbrenner told me to fly Connie and Kirk to New York. Fortunately, the Yankees paid for their flights. They would reside with me in the New Jersey Sheraton for the rest of the season. "The Boss" had a big heart and we will forever appreciate George Steinbrenner! So, they left all their earthly belongings in Tacoma, Washington, even the car! Connie sublet the apartment to another ballplayer and his family.

Kirk felt like "Eloise at The Plaza"! What fun he had being friends with the entire Sheraton staff. He would ride up and down the elevator on the baggage carts and was driven to the laundromat in style! Mr. Steinbrenner took care of our every need. Connie felt like Annie who had met Mr. Warbucks!

During the next few months in New Jersey, we were actually courted by the Mafia. However, at the time they seemed like very generous, friendly folks. Such naivety! Thank goodness our Abba Daddy, God was watching over us. We escaped that web because of God's grace! More about that experience a little later.

The last of the '78 season, we went on a West Coast road trip. When the Yankees went back to New York, they left me in Tacoma to play in the AAA Pacific League Championship to help them win and we did become the Pacific League Champions.

It was at this time Connie and Kirk flew to Kentucky to get her Mom, Rachel, and fly back to Tacoma, gather our belongings, and drive back to Kentucky. I can't say that Connie and Kirk went back home because we didn't have a home. They did have great adventures and wonderful memories on all those trips whether flying or driving. She and Kirk rested at her mother's house until Bucky Dent hit one of the most famous home runs in Yankee history: a three-run shot in the seventh inning of a winner-take-all battle for the American League East title. Then, the packing began!

Line Drive

Have you ever felt like a yo-yo, so many peaks, yet too many valleys? A yo-yo can be up or down every day. This particular year there were too many of each. I didn't know if I was coming or going...literally. Wow, did I start learning how to be patient. The Bible tells me so.

Peter wrote, "The Lord is not slow in keeping his promise, as some understand slowness. Instead he is patient with you, not wanting anyone to perish, but everyone to come to repentance" (2 Peter 3:9).

The Call: "Doyle Second Base"

Okay, I get it, I am supposed to be patient like Jesus. Easier said than done when you are away from your family, plus you don't know where to send them or when you will see them. Here are just a few of the scriptures that helped me.

> *Proverbs 14:29 says, "Whoever is patient has great understanding, but one who is quick-tempered displays folly."*

> *Ephesians 4:2 says, "Be completely humble and gentle; be patient, bearing with one another in love."*

> *Proverbs 15:18 says, "A hot-tempered person stirs up conflict, but the one who is patient calms a quarrel."*

> *Romans 12:12 says, "Be joyful in hope, patient in affliction, faithful in prayer."*

So, it is quite simple that my attitude is either a plus or a minus to me. One of the reasons I am writing this book is to give you hope. You need not lose your joy! Be patient when rough times come. Pray about it and pray for others.

The Call

We live in such a negative world and most do not know that our everyday lives are filled with negative words and actions. Let me explain what I mean by using the example of an everyday worker.

> **Be an energy giver, not an energy taker. WIN!**

To start our day, we shut off the ALARM clock. ALARM is not a positive word. Then the paper is read, or the NEWS is watched. Now, there are not too many positives in the news either. Then we get into a car and FIGHT the morning traffic. Then at work, PUNCH IN. Not positive words. Then it is time to take a morning BREAK, not a positive word. Then a lunch BREAK. Then an afternoon BREAK. Then PUNCH OUT. Then FIGHT the traffic home. Once home, turn on the NEWS. Then end our day by setting the ALARM clock. This is how we are subliminally filled with negativity every day. We need positive energy.

CHAPTER 16

The Call: To Win – The NYY

Welcome to the Yankees, The Bronx Zoo. Graig Nettles had said that when he was a little boy he wanted to join the circus and play for the Yankees. He got to do both at the same time. There is no other team for whom I would want to play. In New York, you always had the call to win, you were expected to win, and Mr. Steinbrenner brought that attitude back to New York.

The hardest thing about the Major Leagues wasn't how good the players were. The hardest thing was being separated from Connie and Kirk. I was called up and down, from the Minors to the Majors five times in 1978. After the third time, I told Connie that she should drive home to Kentucky and stay with her mother, Rachel. She

The Call

thought that it was a good idea. I don't know how many days it took, but I was delighted that she and Kirk were safe in Horse Cave, Kentucky.

Remember when Mr. Steinbrenner brought Connie and Kirk to New York? We stayed in the Sheraton Hotel in Hasbrouck Heights, New Jersey. Most days for lunch we would walk about a mile and a half to a diner. One day a car pulled up to us and asked if we needed a ride to the diner.

I asked, "How do you know that we are going to the diner?"

He said his name was Johnny (not his real name) and that he saw us every day walking there. He told us he always went home for lunch and that his house was on the way. So, the three of us got in his car and he dropped us off at the diner. He also came by to pick us up and took us back to the Sheraton. Johnny was our ride almost every day. I asked him if he wanted some tickets to the game on one occasion. He said that it would be nice. Five or six games, I left Johnny tickets.

One day, the phone rang and it was Johnny on the other end of the line, saying, "Brian, come down and go into the back of the hotel's parking lot, I have something for you. So, I went down and there he was with the trunk of the car open. I gave him a hug and he pulled out three business suits. They were absolutely beautiful. Johnny said that they were mine. I asked him how he knew my size. He said he just checked with the Yankees and got my measurements for my uniform. I asked him how he did that, and he simply said that he had his ways. I asked him what he did for a living and he told me that he was a liquor salesman.

Just a few day later, he called and asked if we could have lunch at his house. We said yes, and Johnny picked us up. Johnny's house was very average, and his wife was really sweet. We had a great time and Johnny took us back to the hotel. Again, I left Johnny some more tickets for several games. A few weeks after we had lunch at Johnny's house, the phone rang in our room. It was Johnny and he was once again in the parking lot behind the hotel. I went down to meet him, and he gave me three more business suits.

I asked Johnny, "Why are you doing this?"

He said it was because I had been so nice to him.

The Call

We made the playoffs and were going to play the Kansas City Royals. The phone rang in our room and it was Johnny again. He told me that he would see me in the clubhouse. I told him that I could not get him in the clubhouse. He said that he didn't ask me.

I just said okay and hung up. I told Connie that Johnny was going to see me in the clubhouse and that I didn't know how he could do it. I got to the clubhouse and in a few minutes in walks Johnny with a few other men. I gave him a hug and we talked a little, then I excused myself to go onto the field. When I got back into the clubhouse, Pete Sheehy (the Yankee legendary clubhouse man) came to my locker. He asked me how I knew Johnny and I told him.

He said, "Brian, stay away from that man."

I asked Pete, "Why?"

Pete told me that he was in the Mafia of New Jersey. My jaw dropped. A kid from Kentucky was so naïve. After the game, Connie and I were walking to our car that was parked in the player's lot. Two men in suits were standing by our car. When we got to the car, the two men pulled out their FBI credentials and said that they needed to ask us some questions. We were scared to death. The questions were all about Johnny. We told them everything. They left saying that he was probably going to try to use me in some way to lose a game on purpose. They were clear that I should never be with him again.

During the World Series, Johnny called again. He said he would see me in the clubhouse. After thirty minutes or so, Johnny walked in with another couple of guys. I walked up to Johnny and said hello and that I was too busy to visit with him. Well, there it is. Two naïve Kentucky folks that learned a lesson the hard way. New York, New York!

With all of that said, being with the Yankees was a blast. There was some type of controversy going on all the time. Billy against Reggie, Reggie against Thurman, Billy against The Boss, Sparky against Billy, oh I could go on and on, but this book would be over a thousand pages. The fans were the most knowledgeable fans that I had ever seen. They demanded wins just like Steinbrenner.

I will never forget the night game when Mickey Rivers was lying on the training table saying he did not feel like playing. There was nothing physically wrong with him, he just didn't want to play. A few of us went in to the trainer's room and said that he needed to get up and get ready to play. We were about thirty minutes from the first pitch. He told a "runner" (we had young men in the clubhouse to do errands) to go tell Billy he was not going to play unless The Boss gave him $5,000.00. The runner went into Billy's office and in five minutes he showed up with an envelope. Mickey opened the envelope and there was a check for $5,000.00!

Mickey looked at the young man and said, "You know 'the N - word' don't take checks. Go tell The Boss I want cash."

Well, less than five minutes later the runner came back with an envelope that was thick with $100-dollar bills. Mickey took out the money and put it in his back pocket. It was time for Billy Martin to walk out to home plate to give the umpires and the opposing manager the lineup. Billy had made two line-ups and we signaled to him that Mickey was playing. Mickey did not come out to his position in center field from the dugout. He went behind the fence and walked onto the field from there.

In the fourth inning, Mickey hit a single. Willie Randolph hit a line drive to the second baseman, and

The Call: To Win - The NYY

Mickey dove back to first base barely safe. The next hitter was our Captain, Thurman Munson. He hit a ball into deep right center field. Mickey was rounding second base and hundred-dollar bills started flying out of his pocket. Mickey stopped and got on his hands and knees to pick up the loose money. Thurman screamed at him to get up and run. Mickey screamed back, "Not until I get all my money!" Mickey was so fast, he picked up his money and slid into home plate safe!

Mickey Rivers is one of the kindest men you would want to meet. He has a smile on almost every second when you meet him. His baseball savvy was unbelievable. He started out with the California Angels. My oldest brother, Denny, was their second baseman and led the Angels in hits in 1974. Gene Mauch was the manager and Denny went up to him one game and said, "Why not put the kid in and see what he can do?" It was Denny who got Mickey in the lineup and a great player was born.

There was something going on all the time because New York is New York. I was usually the first one at the clubhouse. Pete Sheehy was the Yankee Clubhouse Man. Pete was a Clubhouse boy when Babe Ruth played. I

The Call

would go in early and walk around with him as he worked, asking all kinds of questions about past players.

One afternoon I thought I was the only person there. I took off my street clothes and was reaching down into my locker for my sliding shorts. I was butt naked when a spot light came on.

I turned around and there was this lady with a microphone saying excitedly, "I am the first woman ever to be allowed in the Yankee Clubhouse. What do you think?"

Some judge had just ruled that women were being discriminated because men sports reporters were allowed into the clubhouse, but women sports writers were not.

I quickly covered myself and went to the shower room. I gathered my thoughts and went back out with my sliding shorts on and grabbed a t-shirt. The lady asked if I was ready to give the interview and I nodded yes.

Again, excitedly she says, "I am the first woman ever to be allowed in the Yankee Clubhouse. What do you think?"

I answered saying, "This has to be considered a great day for women, do you think?"

With all her excitement, she stated, "Of course!"

I then asked her another question, "Would you consider this being a great day for all women?"

She answered, "Most definitely!"

I said, "Then call my wife and ask her if this is a great day for her."

The light went out and the interview was over. That evening, Connie was watching the late news and saw me wearing only my sliding shorts. She called me and asked what in the world was going on. I told her the story of what had happened. To this day I have packed away a framed certificate from all the New York men sports reporters, stating that on that certain date I was the first "Mooner" to a woman in the Yankee Clubhouse.

Payback

Remember that I had "a thing" about my glove? It always sat beside me and when the players asked why, I would tell them there are two things you cannot touch, my wife and my glove. Remember my first time out to play second base and my glove was frozen with bubble gum in the fingers. Remember that Jim Spencer took my glove, threw it in a mud puddle, and stepped on it grinding mud and water in and around it. Keep that thought.

It was the last month of the season. We were in Toronto and had previously been in Texas. Paul Linblad was a pitcher and was the one who had the idea of stuffing bubble gum in my glove. He had bought a beautiful pair of cowboy boots in Texas. I went to Toronto's clubhouse man and asked if he had any fruit or vegetables that needed to be thrown away. He said he was just about to throw away some tomatoes. I asked if I could have them.

During the game, I went into the clubhouse and to my locker where I had hidden the tomatoes. I stuffed those (almost rotten) tomatoes into Paul's boots. I couldn't wait to see what his face would look like when he went to put on a boot. For the team and me, it was quite a sight to see and hear Paul as he took off the boot. He was so mad that he forgot about the other boot. He went into the shower room and tried to clean the tomatoes out. He was so upset that after putting on the just cleaned boot, he put on the forgotten boot. Wow! It was even better than the first one. Everyone was in stitches laughing so much. Stay with me now. One down and one more to go.

It was the last week of the season. In September, The Boss decided to have jackets made with our name, or nickname and number put on the left chest. Jim Spencer's jacket read "Spence 12." I arrived as one of the first players at the Stadium as usual. I went into the training room and grabbed a pair of scissors. I went to Spencer's locker, grabbed his jacket, and cut out "Spence 12." The only person to see me do this was Pete Sheehy.

That day we had a double-header and Jim Spencer was playing the first game. It was pretty chilly, but because he was playing, Jim did not put on his jacket. Jim was not in the line-up for the second game. He put on his jacket and didn't notice that his name and number had been cut out. When he walked into the dugout, the players started asking what happened to his jacket. Spencer then took his jacket off and saw the hole. He went ballistic. He started going to every player asking if they knew anything about it. Of course, not one of them knew.

He came to me and I just told him, "Sorry." I did not lie because I was sorry that I had to do it to get even. There were six days left before the season ended. During the game, Catfish Hunter came to me and said that he

The Call

knew who cut the hole in Spencer's jacket. He also said that Spencer had put out a reward of $100 to give to the player who told him who had cut his jacket.

I asked Catfish, "Who did it?"

He looked at me with a grin and said, "Brian, you got him back from the first time you were called up and he threw your glove into the mud puddle. It was you who got Linblad back by stuffing tomatoes into his boots."

I started laughing. I told Catfish he had better not tell anyone. He told me he wouldn't. He said that in all his years in pro ball that he had never witnessed anyone waiting a whole season to get back at players. Catfish was impressed.

There were two days left and the season would be over. I heard from other players that Catfish had told Spencer that he knew who cut the hole in his jacket. Spencer had pleaded with Catfish to tell him. Catfish said that he would tell him if Spence would hit a home run in each of the final two games. Spence DID hit the home runs per the "Catfish Challenge"! When he hit the final home run and crossed home plate, Jim Spencer headed directly to my locker where he found it empty. Pete Sheehy had packed up all my belongings for safekeeping. Spence and I had many laughs about this a few years later.

Line Drive

I was very fortunate to play for the New York Yankees. My dream as a little boy had come true. I had to grow up quickly in my first year. However, I had true professionals who poured into me.

Being a young Christian was tough, but having a mentor like Catfish Hunter was a huge blessing. Do you have someone older than you who is your mentor? I really encourage you to have an older mentor. You will grow quicker, and it will make you so much stronger.

Because of the things that I learned, I became a mentor to younger players. The same goes with your spiritual life. Find those that are older than you and be mentored. Then you will find such satisfaction when you become a mentor.

CHAPTER 17

The Call: Can I Play?

Am I Eligible for the American League Playoff?

It was September, 1978 and the Yankees AAA team were in the playoffs for the Pacific Coast League Title. Mr. Steinbrenner wanted to win at all levels, so I was sent back to Tacoma, WA to play in the Championship Series---which we did win. The last of September the Major League Roster can expand from twenty-five to forty players. This gives prospects a taste of what the Major Leagues are like. It also gives the entire coaching staff insights on those extra fifteen players' abilities, and their ability to play under the pressure of New York. So, of

The Call: Can I Play?

course, I went back to New York on the expanded roster. However, things had heated up in the "Bronx Zoo".

We had a very bleak situation going into the last couple of weeks in July. The Boston Red Sox were on an unbelievable winning streak while we dealt with injuries, endless controversy from an alcoholic manager Billy Martin, and an outspoken slugger Reggie Jackson, along with a bombastic owner, George Steinbrenner.

Here are the standings of where we were on July 19, 1978

AL East Division
July 19, 1978

Tm	W	L	W-L%	GB
BOS	62	28	.689	—
MIL	53	37	.589	9.0
BAL	51	42	.548	12.5
NYY	48	42	.533	14.0
DET	46	45	.505	16.5
CLE	43	49	.467	20.0
TOR	33	59	.359	30.0

The Call

The Boss, Steinbrenner, made a major change. Billy Martin resigned in a series we were playing at Kansas City. Earlier Billy had publicly insulted both Steinbrenner and Jackson.

Martin had another of many major incidents with Reggie Jackson, and it eventually led to him losing his job. The game was on July 17 against the Kansas City Royals. Reggie came to the plate in the bottom of an extra-inning game. Thurman Munson was on second base with no outs. Billy put the bunt sign on to Reggie. Reggie fouled the first pitch off, Billy then took the bunt sign off for Reggie to swing away. Reggie squared around to bunt again and fouled it off. Now Reggie had two strikes on him and he had to swing away, but that is not what happened. Reggie squared around the third time and bunted a pop-up that was caught. Billy was more than angry. Veins were popping out of his neck.

After the game, Billy demanded publicly that Reggie be suspended for the rest of the year. However, after talking with all the upper management, Billy reluctantly agreed on a five-game suspension. Of course, Reggie was mad and told reporters he did not know why Billy had suspended him for five games.

To make matters worse for Billy, there were rumors that George was trying to trade Billy to the White Sox for their manager Bob Lemon. Billy had enough, and during a series against the White Sox in late July in Chicago, he spouted out to reporters after the game.

"They deserve each other. One's a born liar [Reggie], and the other's convicted [The Boss]."

Billy, not thinking properly, was referring to Steinbrenner's conviction for making illegal donations to Richard Nixon's 1972 election campaign, a conviction that resulted in Steinbrenner being suspended from baseball for fifteen months.

After the series in Chicago, we got on the plane and flew to Kansas City for a three-game series. I was walking on the second-floor landing of our hotel and saw Billy with dark sunglasses, a sweater tied around his neck, and a crowd around him. I got closer, so I could hear what Billy was saying. He was resigning from his position as Manager of the New York Yankees. He was tearful, and his voice was cracking.

The Call

The Boss replaced Billy with Bob Lemon (Lem). Lem had been fired by the White Sox a month earlier, and no one could believe that the White Sox had let him go since the season before he'd won the American League Manager of the Year. Things began to change. Lem had his first team meeting, said he knew the talent on our veteran-laden team, and we were not out of the race yet. He said his only rule was to hustle every play. We became healthy and the Boston Red Sox began to struggle.

Below are the standings of where we were on Sept. 6, 1978.

AL East Division
September 06, 1978

Tm	W	L	W-L%	GB
BOS	86	52	.623	—
NYY	82	56	.594	4.0
MIL	80	59	.576	6.5
BAL	78	62	.557	9.0
DET	75	64	.540	11.5
CLE	60	78	.435	26.0
TOR	55	86	.390	32.5

The Call: Can I Play?

We made up ten games in a little over a month! September 7-10 became a famous time of Major League Baseball history. It is known as the "Boston Massacre." We went into Fenway Park for a four-game series and completely destroyed them. Fourteen games out of first place in July and tied for first place in September.

AL East Division
September 10, 1978

Tm	W	L	W-L%	GB
BOS	86	56	.606	–
NYY	86	56	.606	–
MIL	82	61	.573	4.5
BAL	80	62	.563	6.0
DET	77	65	.542	9.0
CLE	61	80	.433	24.5
TOR	56	88	.389	31.0

Am I Eligible for the World Series?

We were on a roll as a team. After the "Boston Massacre," we continued to win. The American League East boiled down to the last three-game series. We were playing the Cleveland Indians at home in Yankee Stadium.

The Call

Willie Randolph was the regular second baseman. He hit a ground ball and was running down the line to first base and pulled his hamstring. It was a very bad injury. I took his place. I really felt bad for Willie, but it was the time for me to show what I could do.

It was during this three-game series that Willie Randolph, one of the greatest second basemen of all time with the Yankees, had to sit and watch. All we had to do was win one game and we would be in the American League Playoffs. We didn't win a game and ended up tied with the Boston Red Sox. The Red Sox had beaten us more games than we had won against them during the regular season, so the one game playoff would be at Fenway Park.

The Yankees did everything they could to get Willie ready to play, but the hamstring that he pulled was not responding well to the treatment. Then the call came. Because I had been in AAA playing in Pacific Coast League Playoffs, I was not eligible to play in the American League Playoffs. The rule states that I had to be on the twenty-five-man roster before the roster expanded to the forty-man- roster.

The Call: Can I Play?

The Yankees petitioned the Commissioner and the Kansas City Royals, asking if I could be eligible for the Playoffs. The call came, and special permission was granted as both agreed I could play. What a big relief. I called Connie and she flew to Kansas City along with my parents. It was so good to have Connie there. She more than settled my nerves with her presence. I played well during the American League Championship Series. Seeing Major League pitching for a whole best of five-game series was a big boost. We won the playoffs and were headed to the World Series!

We had a couple of days before the World Series. Connie and I flew on the team's charter plane. I know that she was nervous. She didn't know any of the wives. I saw her interact with the wives and knew that they would love her. They quickly gave her the nickname, Snow White. Connie had raven black hair and a peaches n' cream complexion. They also saw her humility and goodness.

She saw it differently because as we were going up the steps of the plane, she heard one of the wives mention to another saying, "Well this is going to be nice, not many green flies will be around."

The Call

Connie did not know the "baseball" meaning of a "green fly." That term is for people who try to take advantage of a relationship with a player and players would try to get rid of them, but they keep showing up. So, Connie was the nervous one and I was the calm one, because my wife was finally with me.

We had our one day of practice at Dodger Stadium. Willie was trying to run, but he could not. Now the same permission for me to play had to come from the Commissioner and the Los Angeles Dodgers. I kept waiting for the call and I heard nothing from the General Manager or from Bob Lemon, our manager.

The next day, I woke up with nervous energy because of not knowing what was going to happen. Connie and I had breakfast and a restful morning, as restful as I could be. The Los Angeles Times had asked me what I thought of Dodger Stadium's infield playing surface. I was not going to lie and told them it was like playing on Interstate 5. It made the headlines. *Way to go, Brian,* I said to myself, *keep your mouth shut.*

Jim "Catfish" Hunter, my roommate during the regular season, called and said that we would be taking a

The Call: Can I Play?

cab to the ballpark. The one thing that we always did was either walk to or get a cab at least one hour before the team bus left for the ballpark. I loved getting there early because I had time to meditate, pray, and go over in my mind the opposing team and get a personal game plan. So "Catfish," a future Hall of Fame inductee, Yogi Berra, and I got into the cab headed for Dodger Stadium. Yogi started talking to me about an article in the L.A. Times. It was the article about the Yankees and how I liked Dodger Stadium. The writer really ripped me.

Yogi was laughing about it and said, "Shorty, you are eligible and will be in the lineup."

He was just told the news right before we got into the cab. It was only a few hours before the first game that I found out I was eligible. I was so relieved, I felt so comfortable. Our prayers were answered. I felt so grateful. Because of all those feelings, I had a wonderful World Series. I led the 1978 World Series in batting average, hitting .438. I did not make an error, flawless in the field. Sports writers were constantly at my locker asking if I felt pressure or if I was nervous. My pat answer was,

The Call

NO! They couldn't believe my answer, but that was okay because I was having a blast!

I had studied each Dodger player. I knew their tendencies, where they liked the ball to hit, and where they usually hit the ball. I studied each Dodger pitcher. I knew what pitches they threw, what their best pitch was, and what pitch they had a hard time getting over the plate. I was mentally focused.

1978 - Kirk and Connie at Yankee Stadium during '78 World Series
(she was pregnant with Kristin and didn't know it)
The World Series wasn't what was causing nausea.

1978 - Completing a double-play jumping over Dusty Baker

1978 - A great feeling, hitting a double off of Hall of Famer Don Sutton

The Call

1978 - Topp's Baseball Card

New York Yankees Celebration Painting
'78 World Champions

Years later, the *New York Times* asked me to write a piece about playing under pressure. I agreed and started writing that very evening.

What is pressure anyway? When you feel pressure, it is because you do not have control of the situation. To an athlete, this is the exact definition of pressure. It is when you cannot control your nerves, your adrenaline, your heart rate, and you can't control your mind which is saying all kinds of things that are jumbled up.

I wrote that pressure is when you can't pay your bills. I was going to make more money than I had ever made. So, no pressure there. Pressure is not being able to be with your wife and children. So, no pressure there. Pressure is when you are not prepared for the task at hand. So, no pressure there.

> **This was a game that was going to take ALL the pressure off me. I was happy! I was going to enjoy it all!**

My thoughts were, *Wow, I know now how many great players never experienced a World Series.* I knew I had prepared to the best of my abilities. It was like taking a test in high school. If you were lazy and didn't prepare, you took it under pressure knowing you didn't know the material. However, if you paid attention in the classroom, had done all your homework, and studied well you knew you would receive an A. No pressure; you were prepared.

Line Drive

I know that you know it is you who gives yourself pressure. Being prepared takes away the pressure. I remember a parable (a story that makes a point) that Jesus gave in Matthew 25:1-8.

At that time the kingdom of heaven will be like ten virgins who took their lamps and went out to meet the bridegroom. Five of them were foolish and five were wise. The foolish took their lamps but did not take any oil with them. The wise ones, however, took oil in jars along with their lamps. The bridegroom was a long time in coming, and they all became drowsy and fell asleep. At midnight the cry rang out: "Here's the bridegroom! Come out to meet him!" Then all of the virgins woke up and trimmed their lamps. The foolish ones said to the wise, "Give us some of your oil; our lamps are going out."

So, you see, preparation is everything. The foolish were not let into the marriage supper. The bridegroom told them to go away for he didn't know them.

I so desire that you are prepared. If you were to die today, are you prepared to give the correct answer when God asks you, "Why should I let you in my Heaven?"

CHAPTER 18

The Call: To Evangelize

During the American League Championship Series and World Series, Denny and Blake were looking for a city in Florida that would welcome a Baseball School. Our dream was to open a Baseball School. It was perfect timing because Denny had retired, and all three brothers were natural teachers. We were excited about the opportunities.

During the World Series, Blake came to watch when we were in New York. I had a lot of my family and Connie's family there. It was a blast to have so many loved ones there. Blake was able to experience the love and the aggressiveness of the most knowledgeable fans in baseball. He walked out of Yankee Stadium to get on the "family bus" before the NYC police had set up the barricades. The fans swarmed him thinking that it was me. His leather jacket was torn! I had a wonderful game and the fans were so enthusiastic – just wanting to encourage me, just wanting to touch me - that he barely got on the bus unhurt.

Blake went back to Florida to meet Denny. They went to meet with the City Manager of Winter Haven, the central Florida city where Denny had Spring Training with the Boston Red Sox. The City Manager, Jim Easton, was a huge baseball fan and agreed to rent the Red Sox Spring Training site to us. We will be forever grateful to Jim and Cheryle Easton who helped us settle in Winter Haven. We were excited to get the school started right after the World Series.

Tony Kubek, one of the TV announcers for the World Series, met me at the door of our clubhouse. He asked me how my brothers were doing. I told him that they were great and that we were going to open a Baseball School right after the World Series. It turned out to be a great thing.

During the World Series, Tony would say, "Brian and his brothers are opening a Baseball School in Winter Haven, Florida, right after the Series."

We got at least three mentions. Free national commercials about the Baseball School. So, on November

19, 1978, we opened The Florida Professional Baseball School. We had close to 300 students our first week!

1978 - Doyle brothers official picture of opening our Baseball School

1979 - Dad, Robert "Jake" Doyle who started it all!

I had a wonderful off season. It was so much fun teaching baseball. When I returned to Ft. Lauderdale for Spring Training, the very first person that came up to me was Jim "Catfish" Hunter, a future Hall of Famer. He said that he was going to send his son, Todd, to us but did not know how to find us in all the advertisements. I immediately called Denny and told him what Catfish had said. We three brothers decided that our business name had to change to Doyle Baseball School.

During the 1979 season, I couldn't wait to get back to the Doyle Baseball School. At the school, I got "the call" from the Holy Spirit to start each morning with a Chapel Service. Denny, Blake, and I decided to share the Gospel every morning and announce that it was not mandatory to attend. It was a wonderful decision. Most all the students usually attended. Because of my calling as an evangelist, my brothers allowed me to do 99 percent of all the chapels. My studying of the Bible increased dramatically in a different way.

Now I was putting together 20-minute sermons for eight to eighteen-year-olds. At the end of each week, we had a forty-five-minute encouraging time with all the players, their parents, and grandparents. Twenty-five years of chapels saw many decisions for Christ, too many to count. Thirty years later, even as I am sharing with you,

The Call: To Evangelize

I got a call from a former student who wanted to thank me. He was saved at the Baseball School and is now a pastor of a large church. To God be the glory. The call to evangelize every day at Doyle Baseball kept it a source of daily excitement.

Line Drive

We, the Doyle brothers, found out quickly that if you could teach an eight-year-old the right way to hit, field, throw, and run, they could understand and have success. You need to teach the twenty-eight-year-old the exact same way. I found that out in Chapel Service. If an eight-year-old can understand it, then the eighty-eight-year-old can understand it. Keep the TRUTH simple and allow the Holy Spirit to bring in the harvest. It is easy to share the Gospel if you just tell your story of who you were before Christ, how you met Christ, and how you are now after Christ.

CHAPTER 19

The Call: Doyle Baseball

After the five-day schools, Denny, Blake, and I would catch a plane and travel all around our nation. We developed highly successful weekend schools. We did this for ten years and Doyle Baseball became a very notable brand name in baseball throughout the United States. We did not advertise that we were a Christian Baseball School. Because of our baseball educational system, we became very successful. The first ten years, we would have over forty weekend schools a year.

Then, we had the call at the same time. All three of us on the same day said that we needed to train instructors all over the United States and have Doyle Satellite Schools on Saturdays and Sundays. We trained a couple hundred men who did not have to travel a long distance to implement the schools. I can remember having 135 Doyle Baseball Certified Instructors. I would have a father at every Satellite School video all the instructors, which helped tremendously in quality control.

We had four levels of instructors. Level 4 could teach one baseball fundamental very well. Level 3 could teach two fundamentals very well. Level 2 could teach all fundamentals very well. Level 1 was a strong Christian. He could lead Chapel services and share the Gospel of Jesus Christ. All four levels were paid according to their level.

There were weekends where we would have five to eight Satellite Schools on the same weekend. Here is the key. Every instructor said the same thing. There were no exceptions! As an instructor, you had to memorize the terms that were used to teach. The main result of this was the players were never confused. If an instructor did not use the same key words, then he was fired.

Players, parents, and grandparents were accepting Jesus all over the nation. This gave Denny, Blake, and me great satisfaction plus it also gave us more time with our own families.

Since our Level 1 instructors could teach every aspect of the game, they were also invited to instruct at our Baseball School in Florida when we needed extra instructors. We were the first type of baseball business that had a full-time staff. Great baseball men like Jim Zerilla, Rick Siebert, Marv Thompson, Mike Piatnick, Jeff Schugle, Doug Palmer, Ty Coslo, Kevin Malone, and my son, Kirk Doyle. Every one of these have or had professional experience.

> **Doyle Baseball became known as having the first "educational system" that could be taught and understood by all age groups.**

In the early eighties, Doyle Baseball conducted the first Baseball Showcase. We called it The Doyle Baseball Bonanza. Baseball people told us that it would never work. We invited back our best juniors and seniors in high school that had been students earlier in the year. The nation's first showcase had over 250 players and over 200 universities, 50 junior colleges, and over 100 professional scouts in attendance. It was a huge success. Now there are showcases run by universities and baseball organizations around the nation.

Doyle Baseball was known as a baseball innovator. I remember the greatest controversy was that we taught hitting without a stride. The players would go back to their high school and coaches were seeing that their players had become extremely improved. However, many coaches would not allow their players to do the "no stride" approach. It was in the early eighties that I was invited to speak at the American Baseball Coaches Association. This was a long weekend with over 5,000 college and high school coaches in attendance. My topic was "Stride versus No Stride." Many high school, college, and professional hitters use the no stride approach.

We were so blessed to be known as the Doyle Baseball School, where you were going to get a lot more than the best baseball instruction in the world. We were helping hundreds of players find colleges to play. Plus, we were getting some of the best players in the country. In addition, too many to count were now playing in the Minor and Major Leagues.

Doyle Baseball School then became the first Baseball Academy that lasted for three consecutive weeks. These three full weeks of teaching from 6:00 a.m. to 9:00 p.m., allowed students to develop the equivalent of two years of experience in such a disciplined atmosphere.

I grew as a communicator because I had to have twenty-one Chapel Services ready. I cannot tell you how exciting it was to ask the Lord to anoint me with hundreds of messages that were no more than twenty minutes long and that would make a huge difference in players' lives.

Line Drive

Structure and discipline cause one to grow rapidly. Not just in baseball but in life as well. The structure is one's Bible study, prayer, and developing a real relationship with Christ.

Discipline causes one to minister to others. Jesus gave all of Himself away. Discipline gave Jesus complete obedience to His Father, even obedience to the cross. One of the most important things that I can share with you is to "give yourself away." Minister to someone today. Your joy will be full.

The Call: Doyle Baseball

Anytime I feel down, in a life slump, I immediately look for a way to give myself away. Then immediately my down becomes a true upper in attitude, praise, and worship of a living God. That is true joy!

The Call: The Baby Is Coming

June 26, 1979, Kristin was born. It was so great. We felt so very blessed by God to have a son and a daughter! Kristin arrived via a C-Section. The Yankee obstetrician was a dear Irish doctor with a wonderful strong brogue. I was with the Yankees, but I had been sent down to AAA which was in Columbus, Ohio. I gave the doctor all my phone numbers where I could be contacted. I got the call and flew to New York. I went directly to the hospital in Ridgewood, New Jersey where the doctor was waiting.

He came up to me and said, "Brian, my boy, we are going to have to take the baby."

I got on my gown and scrubbed up. As we were walking in, a nurse said that I could not go in because I didn't take the birthing classes. The doctor reassured her that I had.

The Call

Then he turned to me and said, "Brian, my boy, do you have a problem seeing blood?"

I told him that I had delivered calves before, which was quite a bit more blood. I probably shouldn't have compared that experience. We walked in and I kissed Connie. Connie had a spinal, so she was awake.

I remember her saying, "You guys stop talking baseball and keep your focus."

When the doctor delivered Kristin, her eyes were wide open while she was still in the amniotic sac. She was God's gift inside of a transparent balloon. God is so awesome! What a miracle when a child is born. They gave her to Connie. It was such a wonderful sight. The next day, the three of us had our hospital photo in the *New York Times*! Note to family, this was and will be the last time photos are taken and published from our hospital rooms!

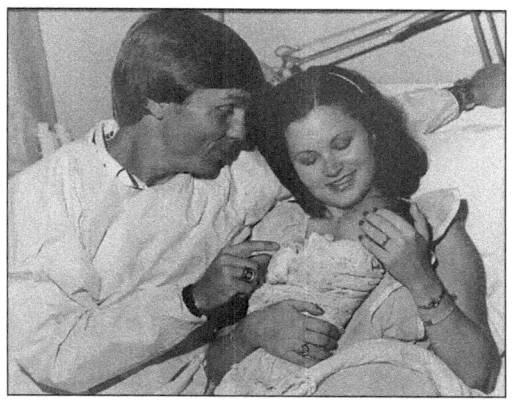

1979 - Kristin only one day old

The Yankees re-called me to the Major Leagues while I was in New York for Kristin's birth. On the day Connie was to come home from the hospital with a four-year-old and a newborn, I had to leave on a two-week road trip. My dad's brother had just died, and Mrs. Payton's sister had just died. Neither of our parents were going to be able to help.

It just so happened Blake called me the day before we were going on a two-week road trip out west. Blake congratulated me on the birth of Kristin. I asked him how he was doing in Rochester with the Orioles AAA team. He told me he got hurt trying to run over a catcher the night before and broke his arm. He said that he was on the Disabled List. He knew about our uncle passing, but he did not know about Connie's aunt passing. I let him know that we were going on a two-week road trip and said that I would pay for his and Jean Anne's travel to New Jersey if they could stay with Connie and the children. He said that they would. What a relief to be able to go on the road trip without worrying about my family.

Once we got back, we had a day off on a Friday. Then Saturday, we were on TV playing the Saturday Game of the Week. Every player lived in New Jersey at that time because the City was having many problems. It took 45 minutes to an hour to get to Yankee Stadium. We all took turns carpooling. Roy White was to pick me up early Saturday morning. He arrived, rang the doorbell, and was really surprised when Blake opened the door.

He said, "What in the world happened to you?"

Now it was obvious to Blake, who had a cast on his left arm from his wrist to his shoulder, that Roy thought he was me. Blake didn't even blink.

Blake answered, "Roy, I was carrying groceries up the steps this morning, tripped, fell, and broke my arm."

At that moment I came from the bedroom and Roy's jaw dropped seeing two Brians. After we had a good laugh, Roy suggested that Blake come to the stadium and play me. Roy wanted to fool everybody.

Blake said there was no way he was going to the stadium, "It is like a mailman taking a walk on his day off."

Roy kept on insisting and finally Blake agreed. When we arrived at Yankee Stadium, Roy took Blake into the clubhouse and straight to the trainer's room. I quietly slipped into the clubhouse and covered myself with hanging clothes in a locker where I could easily see the whole clubhouse and could look right into Billy Martin's office.

Gene Monahan was our trainer and as soon as he saw Blake he said, "What in the world happened to you?"

Blake said that he was carrying groceries up the steps, tripped, fell, and broke his arm. Immediately, Monahan said we had to go see Billy. Remember, we were going to be on TV on "The Game of the Week." Blake walked into Billy's office where Billy was behind his desk eating a "World Famous Chocolate Bar." These were about six inches long with thick squares of chocolate and almonds. When he saw Blake, he bit down so hard he broke his

The Call

bridge! After a few unpleasant words, Billy finally asked what happened.

Blake, without hesitation, said, "Well Billy, I was carrying groceries up the steps this morning, tripped, fell, and broke my arm."

Billy picked up the phone and called our General Manager, Al Rosen.

All Billy said was, "Al, get down here now!"

All our coaches started entering Billy's office. Now, I was getting scared. Maybe this had gone way too far. When Al Rosen came down, saw Blake, and asked what happened. Blake, once again told him the same story.

Billy said loudly, "What are we going to do? Who are we going to call up?"

The gag had gone on long enough. Plus, I might be sent to A ball after this.

I walked in and started swinging my arm up and down and stated, "But, Billy, I can still play today."

Complete silence came over the room. It was as if everyone was in shock or had seen a ghost. The silence seemed like it went on for minutes, but it was only seconds.

Then Yogi Berra blurted out, "Oh, I knew it was him all along."

Everyone burst out laughing. Yogi didn't even know Blake. It was another Yogism. Monahan picked up the phone and called for a dentist to come and quickly fix Billy's teeth. It was fun, but it also had some anxious moments for me. The best actor in the Doyle family became known as Blake, who played the role extremely well. Yes, I was still in the lineup, plus the *Sporting News* ran an article about the whole charade.

> *No faking it because you are a new creature, all things before have passed away, you are new.*

Line Drive

Have you ever played someone else in life? We all have put on false faces. It actually happens all the time. We go to church or a church function and we have a different face and completely different attitude and play the Christian role. Then afterwards we go back to who we really are, which is contrary to following Jesus.

The Call

*When a man or woman **tries** to be a follower of Christ, he or she has already failed. A follower of Christ **is** a follower of Christ. The Holy Spirit (God) lives in them. There is no **trying** because you are a follower of Christ where you are at the time. It comes naturally. Church, home, or work, it doesn't matter the where or the situation. You either are or you are not. I can tell you that being a follower of Christ is a wonderful life.*

CHAPTER 20

The Call: To Be a Husband

1979: As a Husband I Am a "2"

Why is it that we men seem to take a long time to get things right? Is it pride, ego, testosterone, or what? I know that in my life I have been so slow in "getting it." I did not even know what "it" was.

My life might be a lot like yours in treading the "daily grind." I tried to do the right things like make a living so my family could have the nicer things and make things easier. While I was working hard, priding myself that I was working more than 50 hours a week, I was always trying to find a "short-cut" to the pot of gold. I wasted lots of hours thinking there had to be a better way, all the while bragging about my position and how great things were going. After all, I was not a failure, I was successful. At least that's what I wanted everyone around me to think.

"Hey, I'm a man who has everything under control. No one can outwit me. I'm one of the best in my field. It sure would be hard to replace me." All the while, I was the one who was out-witting myself. I wasn't fooling anyone except me.

> **When the final bell rings, what have I got to show for my existence on this earth?**

There comes a time in a man's life where we all have to ask the really important questions: "What am I doing and who am I doing it for?" It is so easy to get caught up in a daily routine that we as men forget the purpose of our existence. Time just flies! Do you remember the boyhood friend you were always going to keep in contact? You and he went off to college and slowly forgot about each other and then fifteen years passed and no contact. That is what most men are experiencing now. We are so caught up in the "rat race" that we can't get in touch with ourselves, much less our wives and children.

The Call: To Be a Husband

Men, we have been slacking in our responsibilities. Our wives have had to take our God-ordained responsibilities and plug up the holes. We are so busy in making a living that we are not living at all. Where has all the joy gone? Why are there so many hassles and problems in our lives? I believe it is because we have given our right to be men away. We think that we are doing our job, but our wives are being men more than we are.

Have I gotten you angry with me yet? Have I stepped on some toes? Well, if you are angry then I suspect I have hit a wound that has been there for a long time and you haven't noticed it.

Take a look around. Do you know what your wife is thinking? On a scale of 1 to 10 with 10 being the best, ask yourself how you would rate your marriage. Then after you come up with your number, see if you have the guts to get the real truth and ask your wife to rate your marriage. Oh, by the way, tell her that she can feel safe with you. Give her that assurance. Why? Because she will be scared to tell the truth if she knows that you would react in a hostile way if she is truthful. Go ahead try it, chicken.

The Call

Do you know what your children are thinking? How much time a day do you sit and talk with them and "really" communicate? *Communication* comes from a Latin root that means listening. Could you say that you give them your undivided attention ten to twenty minutes a day? Do they feel safe in telling you what they really feel?

I remember the day that I was asked to rate my marriage. I thought for a few seconds, carefully weighing the requirements and gave it a "conservative" rating of an eight. I brought home the bacon, I love my children, and I love my wife. Yeah, eight, I know that it is at least that.

When my wife was asked, she blurted out "The Call" and gave a robust answer of two! That's not a number, that's an indictment! How in the world could she embarrass me that way? A two? I should have gotten that rating for just breathing, just showing up after work, just by going to work!

Immediately, I stormed off and started running in the desert. We were on vacation in Wickenburg, Arizona when this marriage rating came to fruition. I started screaming at God about my wife's insensitive rating. How could she have said a two? That is so embarrassing!

"God, why did she say a two?"

God immediately spoke louder than an audible voice, "If your wife thinks that it is a two then guess what it is?"

She has the only and final say. It is I who should love her as Christ loves the church. He gave Himself for her.

So, I told God, "Okay, it's a two. Now what, God? What do I have to do to make her feel it is a three?"

Here is the dilemma, men. I asked my wife how I could get my rating up. I asked her to tell me how to meet her needs. By the way, a great, bestselling book can help all of us in marriage begin to understand and meet our mate's needs: *His Needs, Her Needs* by William F. Harley, Jr.

She gave me an incredible answer, "If I have to tell you what I want then it is not worth me telling you."

Great! I'm supposed to communicate, and she says it is not worth it if she has to tell me. Now, I am not very bright, but I figured that if she wasn't going to tell me I would have to find out some other way. I got book after book. I looked up scriptures about marriage. I read everything that I could lay my hands on. I found out my marriage was a two.

From then on, I have been taking up the S.L.A.C.K. Oh, I haven't gotten to a ten, but I also have always been more than a two. (Since that time, and forty plus years of marriage later, Connie smiles and says, "Jesus is the only ten, but you are next in my book.") I saw where I had been slack, and I purposed myself to take up the slack and am continuing to try to keep the line taut. I thank Dr. Walter Davis for pointing out the S.L.A.C.K.

> **Men Take Up the S.L.A.C.K.!**

Surrender to the Father
Leadership of the Family
Accountability with the Fellowship
Character that is Faithful
Kingdom Focus

What is this thing in me—and in most men—that just doesn't want to go deep into a woman's world? *You are too complicated. It's too hard. It's too much work. Men are simpler and easier.*

Part of my fundamental reluctance to truly dive into the world of a woman comes from a man's deepest fear—failure. Oh, I may joke about "the differences of men and women," Mars and Venus, and all that, but the truth is, I was afraid. What I feared was that having delved into a woman's world, I wouldn't have what it takes to help her. That is my sin. That is my cowardice. And because of her shame, most of the time a man gets away with it. Most marriages (and long-term dating relationships) reach this sort of unspoken settlement.

> *I found out most women do not want to feel alone.*

"I'm not coming any closer. This is as far as I'm willing to go. But I won't leave, and that ought to make you happy."

So, there is this sort of cordial agreement to live only so close.

Some of this simply is selfishness on the part of me as a man. Lord knows men are selfish and self-centered. **When Eve was first assaulted, Adam didn't do**

squat. Men sin through violence and through passivity. It's plain and simple and ugly.

There are plenty of women's retreats. Why? They want relationships. They want answers to help them not feel alone. Women are relational. That is how God made them.

Line Drive

The harder I tried to be a good husband, the more difficult it was. Why couldn't I be at least a seven? Then it came to me, the problem was that I was trying! I looked out at an orange tree and saw that it was not trying by shaking or groaning. It was an orange tree and it produced oranges. I am a follower of Jesus Christ. The more I tried to be a Christian husband, the more it was causing me to fail. I had to learn to just be. When I got out of the way, the Holy Spirit took over and I grew in my relationship with Connie and the Lord. If you know Jesus Christ as Lord, don't try, just be. You will see fruit just like the orange tree.

Water yourself with the word of God. Fertilize yourself by being with other followers of Jesus. Know that you know that you have the Holy Spirit who is now in you. Then you will act and produce fruit. It is so easy yet so hard to be in the way. Get out of the way and just be.

CHAPTER 21

The Call: To Make Followers of Jesus 1980

It was the fall and winter of 1980, and the Doyle Baseball School was doing very well. I was convicted we should have chapel every morning with the students after breakfast and then get on the field to train.

The Call: To Make Followers of Jesus 1980

1981 - Doyle Baseball became the brand for top instruction. Blake, Denny, and Brian

Denny and Blake thought it was a good idea and said for me to write out some messages. Once again, my pen could not stop. This time I had several 20-minute chapels written in practically no time. Sharing the chapels gave me the opportunity to ask if anyone wanted to know Jesus in a personal way. I was always stating that Christianity was not a religion but a personal relationship. We were having hundreds of players, parents, and grandparents making a decision of faith.

The Call

I do not believe in "easy, greasy, slide into salvation" by just saying a silent prayer and raising your hand. I am a person that believes in using Romans 10:9-10. We are to openly confess Jesus as Lord and believe in our heart that God raised Him from the dead. In fact, I would always say, "Don't you dare state this unless you are absolutely sure."

I was excited every week to share the Gospel. The chapels were not mandatory, but very few would not be present through the whole fall and winter. I led the chapel almost every day, so I really grew personally by studying and writing them. I also had the Level 1 instructors who led Satellite Schools around the nation give chapel services that I had written.

It was very obvious to me why God had me with the New York Yankees. The Yankees are one of the most recognized sports brands in the world. Being a Yankee gave me a huge advantage getting people's attention.

Everywhere I would go I always had on my World Series Champions ring. The ring was truly a game changer in my life. Every day someone would ask what kind of ring is that? I would always say it was a World Series Champions ring, and I played for the New York Yankees in 1978. Then I would say you can be a World Champion also by following Jesus. Every conversation was different. However, every conversation was glorifying God.

I distinctly remember getting on a plane from Chicago to Orlando. I had just finished a Coaches and Parents Seminar. When I sat down in my aisle seat, I prayed that no one would sit beside me so that I could stretch out and sleep. The plane door shut, and the seat was empty. I thanked God that the seat beside me was empty. I closed my eyes and began to go to sleep. As we were taxiing to the runway, I felt a tap on my left shoulder. It was a flight attendant who was not working but was flying back home to Orlando.

After the tap on the shoulder she said, "Sorry, but that is my seat."

I got up so she could sit down. She introduced herself and said that she was going home.

I said, "You must be exhausted," trying to get her to say *yes*. She didn't respond. I immediately said that I was exhausted and couldn't wait to get in the air so that I could sleep. Still no response, just a smile came on her face as a reply. We took off and I reclined my seat, closed

The Call

my eyes, and prayed a little prayer thanking God for the wonderful weekend.

Just a few minutes had gone by and I felt a tap on my right shoulder. She asked if I could make room so that she could get some water. I squeezed my legs back and she got out.

She said, "I will get some water for you also."

When she came back and sat down, she handed me the water. I told her thanks and again told her I was exhausted and was going to get some sleep. A few minutes later she tapped me on my right shoulder again!

I woke up and she said in an excited voice, "Is that a World Series ring?"

I said, "Yes, it is."

I turned my head away and closed my eyes. Once again, another tap on the shoulder. I turned and looked at her with a not so inviting look.

She said, "I love baseball. Have you ever seen 'Field of Dreams,' the movie? That is my favorite baseball movie."

I said, "Great," and turned my head to go back to sleep.

Then she said, "You know, my favorite scene in the movie is when the father was walking back into the corn field and asked, 'Is this Heaven?'"

Okay, God, You set this whole thing up, I thought. *You didn't want me to sleep. You want me to witness to this lady. I was in that aisle seat for a reason and You just keyed up the perfect scenario for me to ask...* "Do you believe in Heaven?" We talked all the way to Orlando. Yes, she accepted Jesus as her Lord and Savior.

As we got up to walk out of the plane, she said, "This has been the best flight of my life, thank you!"

God will always give you the opportunity to share His love. Be ready for it. Don't miss it. It is a fastball right down the middle of the plate. Swing!

Line Drive

A professional hitter does not have time to determine whether to swing or not to swing. There is no way to have the time to know if it is a strike or a ball. A hitter must have the mindset that he/she is swinging at every pitch until the ball says stop your swing. I learned that evangelism is like hitting. There is no question that you are going to share the Gospel. Jesus said that we are supposed to share and make disciples. It is not a suggestion. So, just like hitting where you are swinging at every pitch, you are sharing the Gospel until the Holy Spirit says, "Stop, that is far enough."

CHAPTER 22

The Call: Is a Free Agent Really Free?

1980 was a tough year personally. I was in Spring Training with the Yankees and just about a week before we broke camp for opening day of the Major League season, one of the front office "runners" came to my locker and said that Gene Michaels needed to see me. I got dressed and knocked on Gene "Stick" Michaels' door.

I walked in and said, "What's up, Stick?"

He asked me to sit down and told me that I was going down to AAA. I wasn't completely shocked, but was taken off guard. I asked him why. He said I just didn't have the range defensively that they wanted. It was a way to have an excuse for sending me down. The real reason was that the Yankees needed an extra pitcher on the roster.

I gave a little grin to Stick and said, "Okay, if I am going to be sent down then I want to play shortstop every day."

He asked why, and I told him that telling me that I didn't have enough range was a lame excuse and that I had proven that I could play second base and third base in the Major Leagues. Now I wanted to prove I could play shortstop. He agreed to my request. Financially, I was still getting paid my Major League Salary.

During that season, I was sitting in the hotel room in Tidewater, Virginia, the Mets AAA affiliate, watching the Yankees play the Oakland A's in Oakland on TV. Bucky Dent got hurt and Fred Stanley went in to play shortstop. The very next play, Fred went to tag a runner and hurt his hand. I told the guys the phone would ring any minute. Sure enough the call came and I was to get on a plane to Oakland as soon as possible. The Yankees were trying to get me across country before the game ended so that I could play shortstop. I can't remember who picked me up at the airport, but we broke all speed limits to the stadium. I quickly put on my uniform and ran down to the dugout.

The Call: Is a Free Agent Really Free?

The very last out of the game happened. I had just flown from the east coast to the west coast and now the team was flying back to New York City. Unbelievable! I flew coast to coast twice in the same day.

When we got into LaGuardia, I picked up a *New York Post* newspaper and turned to the sports page. The headlines read: "Yanks in Trouble: Doyle at Short." What? This is how I am going to be treated and I haven't played one game yet? Well, I played shortstop for the Yankees and had a very good three weeks. I had two errors, but I hit my first home-run and batted .290. The papers were having to eat their words.

When it was time for Bucky Dent to come off the disabled list, we were in Cleveland. Bucky was in the line-up and I was on the bench. It was the fifth inning of the game and Stick Michaels came into the dugout and said "The Boss" wanted to see me in the clubhouse. This was strange. During the game Steinbrenner wanted to see me? I walked into the manager's office of the clubhouse and there was George.

He started out by saying, "Brian, you have done everything that we have ever asked of you and you haven't

The Call

complained about how we use you. I want to show my gratitude with this new contract."

I looked at the contract and it was a substantial raise.

I said, "Boss, this is a very nice contract, thank you."

George then said, "I want to put a bonus in the contract. Brian, you are a family man, I want to buy you a new van."

Now here is the kicker. Because George was sending me back to AAA after the game, I was thankful that he was giving this contract and bonus. Neither he nor Stick remembered that I was out of options. Meaning that after three years I could become a free agent and if I was not protected, any club could buy my contract for $25,000.00.

I said, "Boss, that is very generous of you, but I don't need a van. What would you say a nice van would cost?"

George said, "Around $20,000 dollars."

I then quickly said, "Boss, instead of a van could you write in the contract that I will receive $20,000 dollars on January 1 of next year?"

George quickly said, "Stick, write that down in the contract and let's get him signed."

So, I signed the contract.

The Call: Is a Free Agent Really Free?

The Yankees were in the playoffs with the Kansas City Royals. I was with the team, but not dressed. I was there just in case someone got hurt. I was in the clubhouse by myself and Billy Martin walked in.

Billy said, "Doyle, you're here for insurance."

I said *yes* and told him that I was out of options and that he could pick me up during the off-season. (Billy was managing the Oakland A's.) Well, that is just what happened. The A's picked me up as a free agent and I was off to Arizona for Spring Training. I had a very good Spring Training, especially batting.

When the season started something happened. I finally got the starting job at second base, but I couldn't buy a hit. I wasn't striking out, but I had no pop to my bat. I tried everything I knew, and I could not hit the ball hard. So, I was being platooned against left-handed pitching. When a right-handed pitcher threw, I was in the line-up. Defensively, I was having an extremely good year.

A Career-Ending Play

However, there was a play while we were playing the Toronto Blue Jays that ended my career. It was a ground ball to our shortstop that was not hit well enough to be a double play ball. The runner on first was Otto Valez. I loved showing how quick I was in turning the double play. Otto was surprised that I was going to turn the double play and he came to second base standing up. He yelled and threw up his hands as he bent down to protect his head. I got up high enough to jump over him except for the tips of his fingers. I threw to first and went head-first into the ground.

Our trainer and Billy came running out of the dugout. I got up and told the trainer that I thought I had broken my collar bone. He felt around and said that he didn't think that I had. Jim Spencer, our first baseman, had the ball. We had turned the double play. So, I yelled to him to throw me the ball so that I could check and see if I could still throw. He threw it to me. I went to throw, and my shoulder went completely out of socket. I fell to the ground writhing in pain. I thought that I was going to pass out. This happened about a week before the All-Star break.

Now the Major League Players Association was in contract negotiations with the owners about retirement issues. We were ready to go on strike. The owners of the Oakland A's were the Haas family, the family that also owned Levi Strauss. Wally Haas was the main family member who was involved with the A's. He came up to me the very next day and said that he was so sorry about my injury. He liked me.

He said, "Brian, you know that the players are going to strike. Let me send you down to AAA and you can keep your Major League salary. Plus, the AAA team will be going to Hawaii in two days. I want you and your family to go to Hawaii on me."

I was shocked. I knew that I could not play anymore that year and he was being more than generous. So, Connie, the children, and I flew to Hawaii to meet the team there.

Is a Free Agent Really Free?

Not in my case. You see, I finally got my chance to become a starting second baseman in the Major Leagues. I was making more money than I had ever made. I was full of myself. Everything was about me and what was happening to me. Even after all that God had taught me, I became selfish once again. People would say that I got a bad break. In reality, God was helping to keep my family together and desired for me to be the godly husband and father that He wanted me to be. Without that separated shoulder, I probably would have lost more than a career in the Major Leagues. I would have lost my family.

Oh, I tried making a comeback. The Toronto Blue Jays picked up my contract and sent me to AAA to see if I could still throw. I was taking two cortisone shots every month just to be able to throw. The Blue Jays released me. However, the very next day the Cleveland Indians picked me up. I played in AAA the rest of the season with them and had a blast because I knew that my playing days were over. I started every game. I hit well, but I just couldn't handle getting cortisone shots in the top of my shoulder and in my armpit just so I could throw. It was time to hang up the cleats and go back to Florida to help run Doyle Baseball.

The Call: Is a Free Agent Really Free?

1980 - AAA Columbus Clippers Family Portrait

Line Drive

I serve a merciful God! I was destroying everything that I had because of pride. I was so full of myself that I didn't have any room for God or Connie and the children. Pride is a very heavy garment to take off. It feels so comfortable. It is so warm and soft, but it is a killer.

Paul told the church in Corinth how someone is to run a race in the right way.

"Do you not know that in a race all the runners run, but only one gets the prize? Run in such a way as to get the prize. Everyone who competes in the games goes into training. They do it to get a crown that will not last, but we do it to get a crown that will last forever. Therefore, I do not run like someone running aimlessly; I do not fight like a boxer beating the air. No, I strike a blow to my body and make it my slave so that after I have preached to others, I myself will not be disqualified for the prize." (1 Corinthians 9:24-27)

The Corinthians knew exactly what Paul was speaking about. Near Corinth was an island called Isthmus where they had the Isthmusian Games. It was something like our Olympics today. We would gasp or laugh if we saw how they ran the race.

> ***Don't make the same mistake.***

The participants who were running the race would walk into the stadium completely naked. They would go to the middle of the infield of the track and stand before the judge who sat in a tower. There they would dip their arms past their elbows in a vat of blood. This would signify that they had trained to the best of their abilities and that they would run the race fairly. Why were they naked? They did not want anything to impede their speed.

When the race was done they would go back and stand in front of the judge in the tower. The judge's seat was called the "bema seat" or judgment seat. There the judge would crown the winner with either a crown of celery or pine needles. That crown would eventually deteriorate.

Paul was telling the Corinthians we are all in the race of life. We will all one day stand in front of the "bema seat," the judgment seat of Christ. There He will give us a crown that will never perish.

What do you have on that would keep you from running the race as fast as you can? I had on the garment of PRIDE. I needed to take it off and I did not. The garment we could be wearing is pride, anger, selfishness, lust, envy, or unforgiveness. We must all take the things off that would hinder our speed in running the right race, not the Rat Race of life. The Rat Race is a race of turmoil and road blocks. We need to be naked before Christ so that the race He has for us to run, we run having been trained and ready to perform *under His rules through the Holy Spirit. I didn't do that during that year with the A's.*

CHAPTER 23

The Call: Let's Do It All!

It was 1983 and I was hearing a call to go do more than Doyle Baseball. I had quit playing and still needed ways to help in professional baseball. I ended my playing career with the Cleveland Indians, so I approached Gabe Paul, the General Manager, and asked if he could use me. It was funny, yet encouraging, to hear him say that he would be an idiot not to hire me. He asked me if I would be the scout for Florida. We decided on a salary and I became a scout. I would leave around 2:00 p.m. from the Doyle Baseball School and go see college or high school games.

It was the end of May that I got the call. The Indians wanted me to manage their rookie team in Batavia, New York. Connie and I prayed and talked about it and we decided I would take the job and that our son, Kirk, would go with me. Kirk was nine and I can tell you that the two of us had a blast. Kirk would help the clubhouse man, plus he would shine the shoes of the umpires. He wanted to make enough money to buy an Atari Video Game System. He made enough money to do that and he felt the rewards of working hard.

My first game day was at home and I went to the clubhouse early, which was not something new. I went to put on my uniform and it wasn't there! I checked with the clubhouse manager and he said he had put it in my office last night. I thought and thought who would want my uniform. I called our General Manger and told him I was pretty sure who stole my uniform.

We had a player who was always looking like he was high on something. One could tell it by looking at the pupils of his eyes. Most of the players were still living at a motel until they could find apartments, so I went to the motel and asked for the manager. He came out of his office and I asked him to please look up the player's name and escort me to his room. We knocked on the door and no one was in the room, so the manager opened the door.

The Call: Let's Do It All!

There it was, folded in a drawer. I took my uniform and went back to the clubhouse. A few of the players had arrived and I went straight into my office and put on the uniform. I put my chair just outside of my door and sat in it. The young man came in and his eyes got real wide when he saw me sitting there in my uniform. I motioned for him to come into my office, and there I released (fired) my first player before my first game as a manager.

I was pretty pumped about the talent that was on the team. I took all the scouting reports and went through each player. We started off really bad. None of the scouting reports matched the players. What in the world was going on? It didn't take long to know that our scouts were doing a really bad job.

I had a pitching staff where no one broke 90 miles per hour, yet their scouting report said each pitcher threw 90 miles per hour and higher. The second-round pick was a right-handed pitcher and he threw his fastball around 86 miles per hour. This was our second-round pick!

I called Gabe Paul and told him our scouts did not know what they were doing. We had one player who had the possibility of going on to the Major Leagues as a

The Call

backup catcher. He had the arm and was 6'2". I worked with him in receiving and blocking. Four years later, he made it to the Major Leagues as a backup catcher.

I remember a night game in Batavia where there was a play by our second baseman on a tag play. It truly wasn't close; the runner was out but the umpire called him safe. I quickly ran out to argue with the umpire. When I got to him the bill of my cap touched the bill of his cap. He strongly said not to touch him, so I turned my hat around. When I turned my hat around, he threw me out of the game. I had not said a word! I asked why he was ejecting me from the game, and he said I was showing him up. I said I was not going to leave. While the umpire and I "worked things out," my entire team turned their hats around as a sign of support to their manager.

I also remember a night no father would ever forget. We were on the road playing the Mets rookie team and the TV weatherman gave an alert that a tornado was headed our way. It was about 1:00 p.m., so I went to every room with Kirk and told everyone to get downstairs under the two stairwells. As I passed one of the last rooms to give the alarm, I looked back and Kirk was no longer with me.

I quickly told the players where to go and frantically ran around the hotel to find my son.

As I was running up the stairs I heard, "Hi, Dad."

Kirk was under the stairs with our catcher.

Kirk said, "Dad, Carlos just prayed the prayer of faith."

I was not only relieved to find my son, but excited that Carlos found The Son. Wow, a child shall lead them. That is what the Bible says, and I saw it happen through my own son.

National Crosschecker

In just four months, Gabe asked if I would be a National Crosschecker. A National Crosschecker was a scout that went all over the country double checking all the other scouts and their best players who had been sent to the Scouting Director. I was known as a very good evaluator of talent.

In 1984, I also scouted, but asked not to be a National Crosschecker. I would go and see a player if Gabe Paul thought it was crucial. Working at Doyle Baseball School and being a scout, I was not at home very much. Even if the game was close by, because it was a night game I got home late. However, the extra income was needed.

The Instructional League

Then manager of the Cleveland Indians, Pat Corrales, asked me to run the Instructional League. The Instructional League is in the fall and lasted eight weeks. Because of the money and since it was in Sarasota, Florida, I took the job. Connie and the children would come by Amtrak late evening on a Friday and go back to Winter Haven, Florida on a Sunday. I was elated to see them every weekend. The kids loved the train and the beach.

I had accepted the job to run the Instructional League because the best prospects of Cleveland's Minor League system were the players I would instruct. I was able to pick my own coaching staff. I had them come in a week early to instruct in their area of expertise. I wanted all my five coaches to be on the same page in every phase of the game.

Five days before the players reported, our uniforms came to the clubhouse. I opened the boxes to see how they looked. I couldn't believe my eyes! They had to be at least five years old and had no names on the back of the

The Call: Let's Do It All!

jerseys. To make matter worse, the hats came from the concessions stand with plastic snap backs and a thin rope across the bill. I was furious.

The reason the Indians wanted me to be there was to teach winning. I came from the Yankees, led a World Series in hitting, and was known as an excellent teacher. Now I got junk to give to the top prospects of the organization? I immediately called Gabe and told him flat out that I quit. He was startled and asked why.

I told him that I was not about to go out on the field with this garbage on me and my players. I said the only way I would stay was to get last year's Major League uniforms, put the names of the players on the jerseys, and get them new Major League caps. I also reminded him of why he hired me and that pride, tradition, and winning could not start unless the players looked like Major Leaguers. I got what I wanted.

After Instructional League, I put on my National Crosschecker hat. I knew what our scouting organization was like. It seemed to me, we had men wanting to make a paycheck, but not caring about doing a good job of picking talent.

The Call

I had been away from home for three straight weeks going as far west as Arizona checking the players whom our scouts were recommending. I had just walked in the door when I got the call. It was Gabe Paul and he quickly said that I had to go see Will Clark of Mississippi State because two of our scouts said that he could not hit left-handed pitching. I told Gabe that I had just walked in the door from my three weeks on the road and could not go. He said that I had to because Mississippi State was playing a double header in two days against Auburn University and two left-handed pitchers were starting for Auburn.

I said, "Gabe, I will go only if you pay for Connie to go with me."

He yelled. I repeated myself. Gabe got angry and said that he had never paid for a scout's wife to go with her husband.

I simply said, "Okay, I quit."

He said, "You can't do that; I will fire you."

I said, "Then fire me because I am not going unless Connie comes with me."

He said in not pleasant words, "Okay, she can go."

The Call: Let's Do It All!

Connie got baby sitters for Kirk and Kristin and we flew into Memphis, Tennessee, rented a car, and drove to Starkville, Mississippi. We arrived at the university and watched batting practice. I went down to the field to talk to Ron Polk, the head coach for Mississippi State, a good friend. I asked Ron which bat Will Clark used. He showed it to me and I picked it up to see the length and the weight.

Let me tell you that a good scout gets all the information that he can get. A lot of times, I would find out who the player's barber was and went and got a haircut to talk about a player. Barbers know character and a whole bunch of other information.

The first game started. Clark never got to swing the bat his first three times. He was not given one pitch to hit.

Connie said, "We have come all this way just to see him walk?"

I told her he could hit left-handers. She looked at me like I was from Mars. I told her it was not only the swing that is important, it is the way you take a pitch as if you were going to swing. Mississippi was losing 3 to 2 in the bottom of the ninth inning. There were two outs and a man on first base. Will Clark came up and hit a ball over 400 feet to win the game. The next game the exact same scenario happened. Clark walked three times. The score was four to two Auburn ahead. Clark came up to the plate with runners on first and second base and hit another walk off home run. I saw him swing three times during the double header. Once was a foul ball, the other two were home runs.

Back in the '80s there were no cell phones and no email. We had to use snail mail to send in our reports on players. A player form had many boxes to check and a section to write comments. I was so mad that I had to go to Starkville just to see that Will Clark could hit left-handed pitching. I wrote on the form, Will Clark, Mississippi State University. I did not fill out any information except in the comment box. I wrote, CAN HIT UNDER WATER! Then I mailed it in to Gabe Paul.

Four days later I got the call. It was Gabe and he was fuming mad. He screamed over the phone so loud that I had to take the phone away from my ear. Of course, he was mad at my report. He had paid for Connie to go and I only wrote, "Can hit underwater."

He screamed, "I ought to fire you right now!"

I explained what I had seen and then said, "Don't fire me, fire the two scouts that said he couldn't hit left handers. They are the ones who caused you to spend the money."

He slammed down the phone. I just started laughing because of what I had heard and what I wrote on the report.

Then came the Major League Draft. All the scouts were in Cleveland. We all came in three days before draft day. Gabe asked me to help run the draft. He knew that I was not happy because I knew the type of talent the Indians had been drafting. I scouted, managed Rookie League, became National Crosschecker, and ran the Instructional League. In addition, Pat Corrales had just asked me to be one of his coaches on the Major League team.

We started the meeting with me asking each scout to get a piece of paper and write down the definition of a Major League fastball. Out of twenty-five scouts, only two had the right answer. I said, "After receiving everyone's answers, this is why the only way we can be on top is to turn the newspaper upside down."

Before the draft many scouts were fired. One scout had even turned in an expense report stating he had stayed at a certain hotel, but that hotel had burned down two years prior. Needless to say, things had to be shaken up. I am a little proud that it was then that the Indians started their turn around and a couple of years later were in the post season.

I did not like being a Major League coach. Players would not listen unless they were playing badly. Spring Training came faster than I wanted it to come. I flew to Tucson, Arizona where we held Spring Training. Let me just say the infielders did not like the drills that I put them through because it was hard work. I had one player say out loud that this was Little League #*#*. I told him that he needed to put some money up where his mouth left off. He was to take 100 ground balls. I, the old man as he called me, was to take 100 ground balls. He caught 86 and I caught all 100, catching the last one behind my back.

I was in the shower when someone came up and tapped me on my shoulder. It was the player I had challenged, and he asked me if we could come out early the next morning to help him defensively. That was the problem with the Major Leagues. You had to embarrass a player before he would listen. I did not go back on staff the next year.

The Call: Let's Do It All!

I had accomplished everything I wanted to accomplish. I had experienced just about every role in professional baseball. It was time to quit.

1992 - DOYLE BASEBALL.

1992 - Photos taken by Orlando's Ben VanHook for a Sports Magazine

The Call

1992 - Serious about instructing

1992 - Reflections after a long day on the field

Line Drive

Even after accomplishing what your desire is, there must be a reason for that accomplishment. I knew that God had called me to work in every level of professional baseball. I want you to know a little secret. My goal was not to work in every level. That was my DESIRE. People get mixed up by stating a goal is an end result. NO! Goals take you to your DESIRE. It even states that in the Bible. Psalm 37:4-5 says, "Delight yourself in the Lord and He will give you the desires of your heart. Commit your ways to Him, trust in Him and He will do it." Goals take you to your desire. Commit your ways to Him is simply giving Him your steps or goals that take you to your desire.

The first word in this scripture is "Delight." Do you remember falling in love and how you couldn't wait to be in the presence of that special one? When you got into his/her presence, there was a lot of delighting going on there. Well, that is how we are to feel when we get into the presence of the Lord. We should feel just like when we were dating our spouse. God desires for you to delight in Him.

CHAPTER 24

Discovering Who I Am Is Not About What I Do

I really had a hard time after my playing days were over. It was like I had lost my identity and was trying to find it. This was before the leukemia diagnosis at age forty. I was in my late twenties and early thirties. I questioned myself a lot. Was I a Christian husband, father, or servant? Was I just going through the motions? Was I truthful with myself? Did I have on the Christian false face? It was a really painful time. The more I tried, it seemed the more I failed.

Connie and I knew that there was something more and we needed a change. We needed to surrender to HIS Lordship. We went to a new church in the 1980s, thinking that it would be the answer. I was trying to find the answer, the missing link, of being the Christian husband that Connie deserved, the Christian father that Kirk and Kristin needed, and the Christian servant that Jesus wanted me to be.

> "A child shall lead them."

The new church was still not filling our need. In retrospect, it wasn't even about the church change. What we needed at that time, and didn't know it, was a godly counselor and life coach! We knew that one of the associate pastors of the new church was leaving and going to start his own church and we followed. The church started out great with sound teaching and doctrine. However, in the course of time, because we are all sinners saved by grace and there is no perfect church, the church doors closed.

We were "church fried" at that point and didn't go to any church for over six months, but our daughter, Kristin, begged us to try one more time at First Baptist Church of Winter Haven. She had found a youth group she wanted to attend. Thank you, Jarrett and Traylor families!

Pastor Ralph Harris so affected my life. He wanted to go out to visit people, more or less, cold contacts, to share the gospel and invite them to church. Ralph asked me to go with him. There were several "Teams" that would go. One of the first homes we visited clearly didn't want us there. The daughters of that family kept asking for the church to reach their parents. Pastor Harris and I went several times and finally experienced a breakthrough with the father of the girls and he became a brother in Christ. The Holy Spirit went ahead of us and prepared his heart.

After a short time, I was teaching an adult Sunday School class. I was ordained as a Deacon, where I had the pleasure of serving many years. I felt the calling to be in full-time ministry back then, but did not pursue that calling. I continued to serve my family and church and minister on the baseball field of Doyle Baseball School.

Line Drive

I truly learned that the more I tried being "The Christian," the more I failed. The pastor of the church that closed was really hard on me. He was my accountability partner and I could not do anything right. I was continually trying, only to be knocked down. It was a very grueling, toxic faith environment. I learned that a ministry or church needs to have a system of accountability. Make sure the church where you attend has good health in every way.

Church leaders are not to be on the throne of our life. That is reserved for Jesus.

CHAPTER 25

The Call: Doctor Says Cancer

Teamwork is the one entity that causes ordinary people to accomplish extraordinary things. The team I was about to become a player on, was something I had never experienced before. As I was walking off the baseball field, I felt very sick and was coughing my head off. The staff of Doyle Baseball Academy was headed to the office to have an end of the week meeting. I really didn't feel like going, but went anyway.

My brothers and I owned Doyle Baseball, so I felt the obligation to be present. I coughed so much, I finally had to go home. That next morning, I went to the doctor and was told that I had pneumonia. Once I recovered from pneumonia, I started having pain in every space of my bones. The first problem was that I started having intense pain in my abdomen. I went back to the doctor and he gave me medicine for an ulcer.

The next week, the pain in my bones and in my abdomen did not get any better. What was really weird is that I started having vertigo. I quickly went to an ear, nose, and throat specialist and he stated that I was having inner ear problems. I was given more medicine that didn't help.

The Rest of the Story

As I shared briefly earlier in the book, my joints were getting so painful I thought that I would go to a friend of mine who was a rheumatologist. Here is the rest of the story.

After having pneumonia, it was not days or weeks, but months before I went to the rheumatologist. Dr. Clement was the first doctor who ordered a blood sample. I left his office that afternoon without a prescription, waiting for him to get back to me.

The next morning at 8:00 a.m., my phone rang. I got "The Call."

Dr. Clement said, "Brian, I need to see you."

The Call

I asked him when and he said, "Now, before anyone gets to my office."

I told my brothers, Denny and Blake that Bruce (Dr. Clement) needed to see me right away. When I arrived at Dr. Clement's office, no one was there. I walked back to his office and when I went in, his eyes were swollen. I knew he had been crying. It is not good when your doctor is crying.

He asked me to sit down. He said my blood work came back and he knew that I had cancer. He told me he had no way of knowing what kind of cancer, but that my blood was in really bad shape. He had already called Moffitt Cancer Center in Tampa, Florida to set up an appointment for the very next morning.

I walked out of the doctor's office, unlocked my car, and sat down with my feet still outside of the car.

I said, "Father, if this is what I have to go through, I am going to ask You to take care of Connie, and I ask that Kirk and Kristin (my son and daughter) know You more intimately than I have known you."

I then put my feet in the car and laid my head back and said out loud, "Father, is this what it boils down to?"

God spoke louder than an audible voice and said, "Son, it is what it is always about, you either trust Me or you don't."

> **Now that is a wakeup CALL.**

At that moment, I felt the peace that passes all understanding. Being in the presence of the Lord, I started to pray for myself.

Quickly, the Holy Spirit said loudly, "You are not to pray for yourself."

Wow, was that a curve ball. There I was knowing that I had some kind of cancer and I was not to pray for myself?

The Holy Spirit said again, "You either trust Me or you don't."

I went home and told Connie the situation and explained how we needed to go to the Moffitt Center the next morning. She was in a state of shock, confusion, and helplessness. I tried to empathize with her, how would I have acted if our roles had been reversed?

I knew that I had better get the people around me that loved me most. God is love so He was first, then Connie and the rest of the family, and of course my church. Our church, led by Pastor Ralph Harris, came and circled our home, holding hands and praying. We will forever be grateful for so many at Winter Haven First Baptist Church—the Harris, Traylor, Owens, Metcalf, Durham, and Phillips families, and the list goes on and on and on.

Line Drive

Through this, I can literally say that teamwork is not just for a baseball game, but for the game of life. As soon as I got my diagnosis, I put together a team. Why? Because teamwork is the one powerful entity that can cause ordinary people to accomplish extraordinary things.

CHAPTER 26

The Call: You Have Six Months

We went to Moffitt Cancer Center that next morning. As soon as we arrived and checked in, I was taken into a room where they laid me on a table, gave me a mouthpiece to bite on, and explained what a bone tap was all about. Painful to say the least. After the bone tap, the doctor apologized and said she had to go in again to the hip, because she had hit a "dry spot" where there was no marrow. After the second bone tap she got the marrow. Thank God!

It was not even five minutes later that a Dr. Spiers came into the room, pulled his chair right in front of me, and said that I had Hairy Cell Leukemia. Connie asked him what stage. He said that it didn't matter, because I needed chemotherapy right away.

I said, "Excuse me, but my wife just asked you a question and you need to answer her."

He told us that I was in the final stage and had approximately six months to live.

I grabbed him by the shoulders and said, "I don't know you and you don't know me. I have one question for you. Are you here to win?"

Startled by my reaction and question, he answered, "Yes."

I asked him, "When do we start?"

He said I was to receive chemotherapy right away and walked us across the hall to start the procedure. He told me that he had already set up a hospital room and that I was to be taken there after the treatment. I was just a little ticked. There was no way that I was going to be staying in a hospital if I had only six months to live.

We drove home after the chemo treatment. Connie called a friend to come over and sit with me while she went on an errand. It was about two and a half hours after the first chemo treatment that my body went into shock.

It was the most uncomfortable and weirdest feeling I'd ever had. I remember calling for Connie and scaring her friend, Cheryle, so that she could not come to the door of the bedroom.

A few minutes later, Connie arrived with two men carrying in a double recliner to our bedroom. When things get tough, the tough go shopping. Connie was not going to have me in any place where she could not hold my hand.

Ten days later we were back at the Moffitt Center for my second treatment. Ten days after that, Dr. Spiers reminded me I had asked him if he was there to win. He informed me we were going to start a chemo program that had never been done before with the medicine *Pentostatin*, which he had invented. I was to take double doses, but it could not be done all at one time. I had to stay in the hospital overnight and take the additional dose the next morning. Again, I told him that I would not be in a hospital room and would get a hotel room.

The next morning, I took the second dosage. After I got home, it was double sickness. I could not walk and had to crawl to the bathroom all night. Thank God, I took comfort from others that I knew were praying for me. It was tough because of the sickness from chemo and the fact that I was getting weaker and weaker.

During that whole time I was going through chemo, I distinctly remember being told that if I got a fever of 103 degrees, I was to immediately get to the hospital. One night, I was burning up. Connie took my temperature and it was at 102 degrees. I asked her to make the call. It was 10 p.m. and our Worship Leader from the church lived only a block away. Connie made "The Call." Our friend Chuck Traylor came over and started praying. As he was praying, I could tell my temperature was lowering. When he left I was at 99 degrees.

I knew I had to eat, but could not keep anything down. Connie would make four or five meals for me at a time, until I could keep one down. I would eat a meal then it would come up. I would yell to her, "It's time to run another sprint," and she would bring me another meal until I finally kept one down.

One Sunday morning, I was sitting in my love seat recliner having a very rough day. I asked the Lord to give me something so that I could really lean on Him. I opened my Bible and it fell to 2 Corinthians 1:3-4, "Praise be to the God of our Lord Jesus Christ, the Father of compassion and the God of all comfort, who comforts us in all our troubles, so that we can comfort those in any trouble with the comfort we ourselves receive from God." I yelled for Connie who was in the kitchen making breakfast to come see me. I shared with her what God had given me through His Word.

Five minutes later, the doorbell rang. Blake had come for a visit. I had a large master bedroom, so if a visitor came they sat at the opposite corner because my immune system was so compromised. A few minutes later, the doorbell rang again. Connie came into the bedroom and went straight to Blake and whispered in his ear.

Blake got up and came over to me and picked me up in his arms. He carried me to the front door where Connie had placed a dining room chair. I couldn't believe my eyes! My church, First Baptist of Winter Haven, Florida had all arrived at my home and were holding hands circled together in my front yard. They began praying for me. God had given me the scripture only minutes before He physically showed me the meaning. What a humbling experience and what a faithful God I serve!

Line Drive

An important lesson I learned from this is that God says when we encounter trials, we are to count it all joy. For God is a God of all comfort and mercy so that when we find someone in the same place, we are to comfort them with the same comfort that He comforts us. Being surrounded by my church praying was so humbling. That day also reminded me of the first day when I went and sat in my car and the Holy Spirit telling me not to pray for myself, I either trust Him or not.

CHAPTER 27

The Call to God: Protect Them

Jesus revealed that God is always at work in us and through us when we allow Him to dwell in us. I was just getting to the point as a parent to begin to experience the fruit of my labors. God was starting a new thing in my life in my relationship with my twenty-one-year-old son and my seventeen-year-old daughter. It was knowing that danger was just around the corner and that your child or children begin to shut you out. There was this feeling of helplessness in my whole being and it even made me nauseous.

Connie and I were going through deep episodes with both Kirk and Kristin. When I say "deep," I mean they both had decisions to make that were going to change their lives. Because of sin that had entered into the very first man and woman, as a verse in the Bible states, we all come to the point where we choose life or death.

The details of their journey are for them to write or not. However, we watched God allow every trick of the enemy to serve as a learning curve to strengthen our faith in Him. God, in His faithfulness, continues to get the glory in our lives every day. May you be encouraged no matter the weight of your present battle.

Line Drive

You find yourself helpless when one or more of your children are making wrong choices. Connie and I were constantly on our knees praying. We were claiming God's protection over them. We were praying God's word and His promises over them. It is scary to let go, but parents must learn to let go and give their children to Him because He loves them more than anyone.

Yes, we would die for our children. However, God sent His Son to die for them. Don't be afraid to pray that God will bring circumstances and situations that would bring them closer to Him. Also, pray that He will bring people around them to influence them to have a close relationship with Christ. He will do it.

CHAPTER 28

The Call: Downsize to Build Up

1999-2001 Listening but Not Hearing

Have you ever known what you must do but you can't do it? Well, that is the position I found myself in during the late '90s and early 2000s. I knew that God was calling me into full-time ministry, but I was not listening. Maybe I was listening, but not hearing. Do you know what I mean?

Oh, I was ministering every day. If it was not at the Baseball Academy, it was through the church. I did not do either one because people expected me to. I did it because I had the passion and joy in ministry. The Holy Spirit, in His quiet voice, would say to me it was time for me to leave the Baseball Academy and enter full-time ministry.

The Call: Downsize to Build Up

During the late '90s, Professional Athletes Outreach had a long weekend for Major League Baseball players and their wives to get away and hear powerful speakers and have breakout sessions. My future partner in the MLB Agent business, Bill Rose and his wife Vicki, invited us to come for the weekend. The main speaker was Joe Stowell. Another speaker was Dave Dravecky along with his wife, Jan.

Dave was a Major League pitcher who had broken his arm while throwing a pitch in a game. They x-rayed the arm and found cancer. To save his life he had the arm amputated. Their message mimicked what Connie and I had experienced in our lives. It was uncanny. Everything they had gone through and were going through was like they were talking about us. The difference was, we were going through it without the answers. They gave us some answers. After their session, Connie and I broke protocol. I went alone to talk to Dave and Connie went somewhere with Jan.

We left that conference with lots of joy, but still had lots of questions and "what ifs." We went back to Winter Haven to do what we always had done. I continued to conduct the Doyle Baseball Academy. The only thing that was different was now we became "empty nesters." We sold our house to a Cleveland Indian player and moved into a townhouse.

God was still calling me into full-time ministry. I was listening but not hearing. Listening is hearing the noise. Hearing is understanding the words that are being said.

9/11/2001 Changed Us All

It changed me to think about what I had gone through, but more importantly where I was going. Our immortality became even more real. Immortality is a wonderful word. To live forever with Jesus is so exciting to me. However, each of us needs to look at that word carefully. Because if you take out the "t" (the cross) then you get immorality. We need to bow at the foot of the cross of Jesus.

I had the strong desire to finish my life STRONG! I began to evangelize with even more fervor using 9/11 as an example of our temporary time on this earth. In saying that, as I was finishing the writing and editing of this book, evangelist Billy Graham went home. Perhaps you

The Call: Downsize to Build Up

know this story about Billy finishing strong. Enjoy this excerpt from O.S. Hawkins book, *Rebuilders Finish Strong*.

Billy Graham started his ministry in the mid-1940s, and at the age of twenty-seven, began to gather crowds in his preaching services. However, has anyone heard of Chuck Templeton or Bron Clifford? In William Martin's biography of Billy Graham, he says that Chuck Templeton was "the most gifted and talented young preacher of his era." Billy Graham, Chuck Templeton, and Bron Clifford were all young preachers of renown in the mid-1940s. Many authors have recounted their stories, but none better than my friend Steve Farrar in his volume entitled *Finishing Strong*. In 1946, the National Association of Evangelicals published an article entitled, *The Best Used Men of God*. The article highlighted Chuck Templeton and made no mention of Billy Graham. When Bron Clifford was twenty-five years of age, he was preaching to thousands of people. Everywhere he went there were overflow crowds. It is reported that by the age of twenty-five, he had touched more lives and set more attendance records than any clergyman in American history. He was tall and handsome, intelligent and eloquent. In fact, he had opportunities from Hollywood producers to play significant parts in many of the Biblical movies that emerged in the late '40s and early '50s.

"Yes, we have heard of Billy Graham, but whatever became of Chuck Templeton and Bron Clifford? Chuck Templeton left the ministry to pursue a journalistic career and by 1950 was reported to no longer believe in the Lord Jesus Christ in what one might call the orthodox sense. In 1954, Bron Clifford lost his health and family, and became an alcoholic. At the age of thirty-five, this great preacher died in a rundown hotel room on the outskirts of Amarillo, Texas, of cirrhosis of the liver."[1]

---

[1] http://oshawkins.com/sermons/rebuilders-finish-strong/

The Call: Downsize to Build Up

When asking yourself about living a purpose-driven life for Christ and finishing strong, consider your answers to these questions:

Why are you here living?
What is your purpose to be alive?
On a scale of one to ten, how happy are you?

A lot of times, the people that I spoke to did not identify those questions as "spiritual questions." I was able to explain why they were living and breathing and why they had a purpose. I was not only traveling for baseball clinics at this time, I was also scheduled by churches to conduct evangelistic events or a men's retreat.

I remember that I was booked in Ft. Lauderdale, Florida, for an event they held every month. It was a power luncheon for the downtown businessmen. Dr. Larry Thompson was the Lead Pastor and asked me to come. As we were walking from his office through the sanctuary, I noticed a lot of building going on. I asked him what was going on and he said that the stage was getting ready for their Christmas Pageant. I asked him to explain. They held twenty-one performances and had won five Emmys. Many people came to Christ in those twenty-one performances.

> **Again, I missed what God was calling me to do.**

After the luncheon, Dr. Thompson made a peculiar statement, "Brian, I want you on my staff."

I quickly said thank you, but I was able to preach every day and see souls come to faith. As an evangelist, I could not see myself on a church staff. We left it at that. I said quickly that I would not become a full-time pastor.

Line Drive

Have you ever missed the Holy Spirit's voice? Can you recognize His voice? I know His voice by two methods. First, I have a tingling down my spine and I get "chicken skin," or goose bumps.

Secondly, in almost every case when the Holy Spirit speaks, He goes against everything my flesh wants to do. I have learned to answer His calling first before all things.

How does He speak to you?

CHAPTER 29

The Call: It's a Brand-New Game

In 2002, I had gone into partnership with Bill Rose creating a Major League Sports Management Agency. I was to get the talent and he was the businessman. Bill was also a small minority owner of the New York Yankees. Let me say something here, even if you are a small minority owner of the New York Yankees, there is nothing small about that.

Bill is a loving Christian man with a loving Christian wife, Vicki. They have two children; the youngest, Courtney, and the oldest Douglas. It was Douglas that caused us all to be very good friends. Douglas came to our Baseball Academy when he was very young and continued through his high school career.

The Call

Our son's wife, Amy, was pregnant with their first child. It was going to be a boy. Bill wanted me to go to Japan to scout their High School Country Tournament and to watch their professional league players. Kirk joined me to help, not just in scouting, but to help me get from one place to the other. My joints were bad, and I needed someone to help. What a sight to see watching Japan's High School National Championship Tournament. Their respect for the game is second to none.

When we arrived back into the states, it was only a few weeks and our first grandchild was born. Parker Reed Doyle. How wonderful it is to have grandchildren! Yes, I said grandchildren because I have a total of five wonderfully spoiled grandchildren. Grammy and Granddad have that privilege.

Why did my story go from our trip to Japan for our new MLB player agency to our first-born grandson? Because at four years old, Parker had cancer on the back of his head. It was Bill and Vicki Rose who became our family's armor bearer. Flights, hotels, meals, and anything that we needed was provided through the Roses. Even the specialist at Boston's Children's Hospital. Bill found us the best.

Parker had nine surgeries, hospital visits for saline injections, and two infections. This experience started when Parker was four and was finished at age six. Grammy Connie was continually flying to Boston to assist Amy, Kirk, and Parker. Nana poured out her love on the sibling grands, Payton and Paris. Our God is so good. Parker is cancer free and playing sports. He is crazy about baseball and is a very good player.

Line Drive

Here was another wake-up call. Prayer was the only thing that the entire family had. Our knees were sore. Our God was soaring. Jesus is sitting on the right side of God, His Father, always making intercessions for us. I truly believe that. Why? Because I have had many experiences that prove He is faithful. That is a TRUTH, not a fact. Facts change, TRUTH never changes.

CHAPTER 30

The Call: I Had to Answer

I was still working at the Baseball School and with Bill Rose as a player agent. The firm was named DRM, which stands for Doyle, Rose, and Middlebrooks. Then after three years the "M" stood for Moye. Mike Moye was gracious enough to become a partner. He had been an agent for many years and was considered the best lawyer for arbitration in baseball. I was traveling and setting up scouting workouts for candidates.

I was busy, however, I was still hearing the call to be a full-time minister. There was no way that I could justify in my mind that becoming a pastor would shackle me from doing what I love—evangelism and teaching. I was doing that at least five times a week.

The Call: I Had to Answer

We were living in Central Florida. In fact, we lived in Winter Haven, Florida, for twenty-five years. During that time, I was the On-Field Coordinator and Curriculum Developer for Doyle Baseball Academy. I was extremely busy at Doyle Academy, DRM Agency, and with our church.

More and more I had sleepless nights questioning God about being called into full-time ministry. Every day it was on my mind.

I started talking to Connie about it and she was a little frightened about being a pastor's wife.

Where would we go?
How would I be ordained not having a seminary degree?
I did not have a college education so how could I go
to seminary?

However, our faith said if that is what God wants, then let's go for it. God doesn't worry about obstacles. If it was to be then it will be.

Line Drive

We see obstacles instead of opportunities. Our life is like a vapor. We are here today and gone tomorrow. I was truly thinking about my immortality. I still had the competitive edge running in my soul.

If I were to be an ordained minister, then it had to be God. There are times when I really know that it is the Holy Spirit speaking to me because my flesh does not want to obey Him.

Does your flesh get in the way of hearing from God? Surrender right then and go do what our Heavenly Father wants you to do.

CHAPTER 31

2004 Year of Jubilee
The Call: Obeyed at Age 50

I was now cancer free. I knew I had to answer the call to full-time ministry. I called just about every pastor I knew and had spoken in their church. I asked each one about being ordained at age fifty.

Every pastor that I spoke to said, "It's about time you are obedient."

So, I went to my pastor, Dr. Walter Davis, and asked him what he thought about the matter. He also said that it was about time to answer the call. He said that he would be honored to ordain me. I was excited and nervous at the same time. Dr. Davis told me that I had better start studying and praying because the ordination was on his shoulders. He clearly meant that he would someday stand before God and give an account of his ministry and a part of that would be who he ordained into the ministry.

The day came for the questioning, a Sunday afternoon. Dr. Davis had asked many pastors to be present for the questioning. I was drilled for 2 hours and 45 minutes. I had to answer their questions without a Bible.

Believe me there were pastors present who seemed to be there to make sure that I did not get ordained because I had not been to seminary. However, when questions started flying, the Holy Spirit was all over me. It is hard to explain (who can explain God?), but I answered every question.

They asked me to leave the room and they discussed my capabilities. I was called back into the room ten minutes later. I thought, *Oh no, that was too quick. There is no way I am going to be ordained.* I stood in front of all these men and Dr. Davis spoke.

He said, "Congratulations, Brian, it was unanimous that you become an ordained minister of the Southern Baptist Denomination."

I was happier than when champagne was being poured on my head when we won the World Series. The ordination ceremony was scheduled for Sunday evening. I told Connie the news and we cried and rejoiced at the same time.

Fifty years in the Old Testament is the Year of Jubilee. That is exactly how I felt. The ordination ceremony was awesome. It definitely was a spiritual stake in the ground. One of the most awesome things during my ordination was that Dodie Davis, Dr. Davis's wife, sang "Joy in the Journey" by Michael Card. Everything I had gone through, the hearing but not obeying God, the leukemia, the hard times both of our children went through, and the anticipation of the future of being a pastor made that song perfect.

Line Drive

After all the trials and tribulations that we had gone through, it reminded me of the trials and tribulations that Israel was told were going to happen. Then in Jeremiah 29:11 it says, "For I know the plans I have for you," declares the Lord, "plans to prosper you and not to harm you, plans to give you hope and a future."

CHAPTER 32

The Call Out: God Help!

I was now an ordained minister. What was I going to say to my brothers Blake and Denny? I had been with them for twenty-five years. Now I was going to be telling them that I would be moving wherever God wanted.

I could not face the two of them at the same time. So, I went to my twin brother first. I gave him half of my stocks and told him what I was going to do. I asked him not to call Denny because I was going directly to his house after I left Blake's. I gave Denny the other half of my stocks and told him what I was going to do.

I went back home and walked into the house and said to Connie, "Well, are you ready to go to Minnesota, Wyoming, or any place God tells us to go?"

The Call Out: God Help!

She said *yes* and we both started crying. Our world was about to change drastically. We prayed and asked God for help. Thirty minutes passed, and the phone rang. It was Dr. Larry Thompson who had asked me to be a part of his staff in Ft. Lauderdale. It was that same man I had told it would never happen because I loved ministering every day at Doyle Baseball. He said that he had a position open and would I consider taking it. The position was Pastor of Evangelism and Pastoral Care. I told Larry, "Thank you," but I needed a while to pray and think about the position. He said for me to take the time and give him a call.

Well, we knew quickly that we were to go to First Baptist Church of Ft. Lauderdale, Florida. This is a church of 15,000 members. Wow, did we need God's help.

On the way to Ft. Lauderdale, following our moving truck, I got a call from the Education Pastor, Kevin Ellington. He informed me I was going to be the Senior Adult Pastor along with the other responsibilities. Immediately, I wondered how many that would be because of the overall membership. Secondly, Connie and I had taken three or four spiritual assessment tests and I had scored a zero on mercy in each of them.

The Call

How was I going to be the Pastor of Senior Adults when it was hard to walk in mercy?

We arrived around 3:00 p.m. and I was to go to work by leading an evangelism class that evening. I was in ministry. Because of the scope of each of the three ministries in which I was in charge, Connie and I had to yell, "God help!"

God in His mercy was in control. I got out of the way and watched Him put things together. Dr. Larry Thompson is such a good leader. When we went there before I was hired for an interview with staff members, the Executive Pastor, John Jones, asked me what I perceived to be my salary.

I think that I shocked everyone at the table when I said, "God has put me here and I will not state what I think my salary should be. That is up to God and you."

Looking at their faces, I don't think anyone had ever said that to them.

After my first evening in teaching evangelism, the very next day I received a call from a lady named Debbie Corsini.

We serve a good God.

The Call Out: God Help!

She asked if Connie and I could have lunch with her at the Olive Garden. She wanted to discuss something with us. When we met with her, we could see the passion she had about helping others, especially care-givers. She came up with the name, Caregivers Connection. Once a month all the caregivers would meet at the church for a break and learn from each other's experiences. It was a huge success. I told her she had my full support and to start as soon as possible.

Ft. Lauderdale is a beautiful place. It is also a fascinating city spiritually. There were several big churches in the area and yet 85 percent of the population was unchurched. For me that was very exciting. Being an evangelist, there was more than enough work for me. I loved serving in Ft. Lauderdale because spiritually speaking there are no gray areas. It seemed as if the "light" was lighter and the "dark" was darker. We are so thankful for all His light in South Florida and the world!

2005 - Answering "THE CALL" at First Baptist Chuch Ft. Lauderdale

Connie and I designed this tile that is still on The Wall at FBCFL. 2 Corinthians 5:17 New Life represented by the butterfly flying out of the broken baseball

Better still was their famous Christmas Pageant. The Pageant was performed either nineteen or twenty-two times, depending on the calendar. There were over 2,000 people involved. It won five Emmy Awards.

People would hand in their written commitment to Christ and I would tally the decisions. Then I trained people what to ask and how to minister to these seekers for the follow up.

> *Jesus is the steering wheel, not the spare tire.*

First Baptist Ft. Lauderdale and Dr. Larry Thompson hired me to do a job. He never micromanaged me. He gave me complete ownership of my ministry. He allowed the Holy Spirit to work with me uninterrupted. Because of this, when Connie asked what my favorite job was, I quickly said that it was pastoring at First Baptist because of Larry Thompson and the people there.

Line Drive

How many times have you yelled or prayed, "God, Help?" He is our very present help in times of trouble. The secret is to take your hands off the steering wheel of your life. Allow God to take control.

Sometimes I see people treating Jesus as a spare tire. You never think about the spare tire in the vehicle until you need it. I pray if that is how you think, then change it right now.

CHAPTER 33

The Call: Safe at Home

Family

Connie and I have five grandchildren. Kirk and his wife Amy's children are Parker, sixteen, Payton, fourteen, and Paris, twelve years old. Kristin and her husband Trevor have two children: Tyson, eleven and his sister, Reagan, nine years old at the time of the writing of this book. Why do grandchildren grow up at warp speed?

Kirk lived in northeast Alabama where Amy grew up when I was pastoring at First Baptist. Kristin was at Liberty University when I started at First Baptist. In fact, Kristin and Trevor were married at First Baptist Ft. Lauderdale. Eventually, they moved to Newnan, GA.

The Call

When Reagan was born, Kristin noticed something odd with her left eye. She immediately went to the doctor. In her second week on this earth, Reagan had eye surgery. Reagan was born with a condition called Persistent Hyperplastic Primary Vitreous (PHPV) resulting in a vision impairment.

With Parker having cancer, Payton having surgery because he was born with a pin-hole in his throat, Paris having severe bouts of UTI's, and now Reagan born with PHPV, it was time for us to move to Georgia to help!

At first I thought, how are we going to make a living going to Georgia? I was very hesitant. You see to live in South Florida is very expensive. My first five years there as a pastor at First Baptist and being a Major League Baseball Player Agent, I did not have one day off. After five years, I finally started taking Mondays off. Connie was ready to go to her grandchildren, period!

Close friends of ours, Dave and Linda Mitroff from Chicago, knew that I was a workaholic and bought tickets for Connie and me to go to the Caribbean with them for a week. They rented a home with a chef. It was not just wonderful, it was fantastic! The next to last day there,

Connie wanted to talk about moving to the Atlanta area where we could be close to both Kirk and Kristin. They both had asked us several times to move there. They not only needed us there, they truly wanted us there.

I was very hesitant. Connie and I had a "discussion." She left and started walking up the mountain where the house was situated. I sat at the pool praying. I got the answer. I walked after her and there almost at the top was Connie. I told her she was right. We needed to move to Georgia. She was elated.

However, I had some conditions. I was starting a new program at First Baptist. It was Neighborhood Groups (Home Bible Studies). I had to get that off the ground and running smoothly. Connie understood and after the vacation, she flew to Atlanta and went to Newnan, GA, where our daughter lived to look for a home to rent. There was really nothing on the rental market that met our needs. Also, renting and buying cost practically the same.

I took a weekend off and flew to Atlanta. Kristin picked me up and I went with Connie to look for a house to buy. We only found one home that might work. We put a bid on it and the bid was not accepted. Connie stayed with Kristin and I flew back to Ft. Lauderdale. A few weeks later, Connie came back to Ft. Lauderdale.

As we were driving back to our apartment, we got a phone call from Kristin. She said that they had found a house for us. They explained it, told us they had met the neighbors, and sent pictures of it. It was a foreclosure. We put in a bid unseen and the bank accepted it. We bought a house without seeing it. We flew back the next Friday and closed on the house. I left Connie there and went back to Ft. Lauderdale. Connie found a female contractor who had reinvented herself. Instead of building homes, she renovated foreclosures. So, Connie started renovations with the contractor and felt right at home because of our neighbors, John and Evelyn Pollock, who have become close friends.

I stayed a year at First Baptist before I moved to be with my family. God had not released me yet to leave the ministry that He had me start. I had to finish it before I could leave.

I wrote my letter of resignation and handed it to Dr. Larry Thompson. We had talked about retiring together. He was very understanding, knowing all the health issues of our grandchildren. The time came for my last Sunday at First Baptist. The whole Church treated us with such respect and threw us a giant going away party. It was absolutely awesome. When a pastor has to leave a church, this is how it should be, a celebration of thanks.

> **So, Connie and I moved to Newnan, Georgia.**

Line Drive

I knew that I knew I was to stay at First Baptist Ft. Lauderdale to finish the work of developing Small Groups. These were to be Neighborhood Groups that met in a home to study the Bible. The church had the traditional Sunday School, but God also desired for the church to have an outreach ministry to people who do not go to church but would meet in someone's home.

Have you ever felt that there was a place you were supposed to go, but could not until something was finished? Most of the time we make decisions with our emotions or "our feelings." It was hard to stay in Ft. Lauderdale while Connie was in Newnan. However, we all need to be still and listen to the

The Call

Holy Spirit to hear what God desires. Because of being obedient to God and staying to finish the work that was started, we were blessed by the church's send off. Waiting is difficult but so worth the wait.

CHAPTER 34

The Call: Mission Work

God blessed us with a wonderful home where the grandchildren could stay and where we could help missionaries of First Baptist Church of Ft. Lauderdale when they were headed to and fro.

When I walked into the house, Connie said, "Welcome to our missionary home."

Little did we know what was going to happen and how our lives were going to change.

Connie and I were praying about what God wanted me to do. Should I start putting out my resumé? Should we start a church with Trevor, my son-in-love, as the lead pastor and me the executive pastor?

The Call

It was thirty days later that I got the call from a great friend, Jeff Siegel. Jeff and I had been accountability partners for over fifteen years. Jeff had been a Doyle Instructor for me. I remember the day I told Jeff he was going to be a Level 1 Instructor. This meant that he was to be the leader of a weekend Satellite School.

Jeff held his first Chapel Service on a Sunday afternoon and he saw over forty people come to faith in Jesus Christ. It literally changed his life. He was a manager at a company called Service Master with a good salary. Jeff decided to leave his job and start a ministry called Global Youth Baseball Federation, Inc. In 1997, he started going all around the world teaching baseball and sharing Christ. It was August 2000 when Global Youth Baseball Federation, Inc., became a 501(c)3.

I got the call in August of 2011, Jeff said, "Brian, Israel is ready."

I said, "Explain what you mean that Israel is ready."

"Israel is ready for you to write a baseball curriculum for their University of Athletics (Wingate Institute), and it's time for you to become part of the staff of Global Baseball," he said.

In Israel and some European countries, one must take college classes to coach. For instance, if you want to coach six- to twelve-year-olds, you must take 100 hours. If you want to coach thirteen-year-olds and older, you must take 170 hours. If you desire to be a national coach, you must take 250 hours.

So, I wrote an AA Degree, a BA Degree, and a Master's Degree in Baseball Coaching. Israel wanted the curriculum, but they said they were leery that I would share my faith in Yeshua (Jesus). Jeff explained to me that I could share my faith with eighteen-year-olds and older if it was a one-on-one conversation. I told him that I understood.

Because of the written curriculum, Global Baseball is able to use it in nations like Ecuador, the Dominican Republic, Cuba, Kosovo, Austria, and Spain. Uganda has made a special request for a National Baseball and Softball curriculum with coaches going with equipment to work with grade school through university students. There are still many nations that desire the teaching.

Cuba is a fantastic ministry opportunity. Jeff Siegel, President and Founder of Global Baseball, started going there fifteen years ago. The government saw that he had no interest in politics. They watched him bring in humanitarian aid and teach baseball to less fortunate children. Government officials called him into their headquarters called "The Revolution Square." They told him that he proved to them that he had no interest in politics and saw his love for the people and children of Cuba. The head of Religious Affairs told him that they had no problem with his belief in Jesus and his desire to plant churches. They explained that because Jeff was honorable, religious visas would be granted for anyone he would bring to help with the ministry in Cuba.

The Department of Religious Affairs gave him permission to plant churches anywhere on the island of Cuba. They just asked for additional help with humanitarian aid and construction on homes that needed repair from hurricane damage.

Jeff works with a pastor named Eduardo who started four house churches east of Havana in a city called Alamar in 2001. With the help of Global Baseball, there are now one hundred and ten house churches.

The main ministry center in the city of Alamar has three houses and the ability to house over one hundred people. This includes three meals, hot showers, and air conditioning. Funds that used to be spent in broken-down government hotels are now utilized to create jobs for cooks, housekeepers, security people, interpreters, construction workers, and leadership.

I went to Cuba with Jeff to minister to house church leaders. We visited a house across the street from the main church house. The lady who owned it was told about the good work that Global Baseball was doing with children. She said that she wanted to sell it to Global Baseball. This came from a recommendation of a neighbor who gave his life to Jesus. Global Baseball purchased the house, remodeled it, and gave it to the church in Alamar.

God has really blessed our ministry in Cuba. We started youth leagues and each coach is a member of one of the house churches. Athletic teams and church groups go to Cuba with Global Baseball and are part of a holistic approach to ministry. Sports are the main platform for Global Baseball, just like humanitarian aid is for Franklin Graham. Once we are in a country, we see additional opportunities through medicine, music, humanitarian aid, aviation, and additional sports.

The Call

Jeff and I have become friends with some very important government officials. Some close friends of Fidel Castro have accepted Christ. I cannot use their names, but it was truly the Holy Spirit that was present each time we shared. What a humble thing to share Jesus Christ with men and women who have contact with such high government individuals.

The last time I visited Israel, the man who is involved with building the third temple wanted to meet with Jeff and me. Jeff had known him for several years. His name is Gershon Solomon and I had so many questions about the temple. I asked him and he graciously answered each of them. Then he asked me if I believed that Jesus is the Son of God and I said yes.

He spread out his arms and with a loud voice said, "Brian, you are an abomination to God. How could God live in stinking human flesh!"

I said, "Gershon, pull out your Tenach and I can show you why."

He said, "I don't need to get the Tenach (Torah, Prophets, and Writings). I know the Tenach."

I told him that I did also, but I asked him if he would appease me.

Jeff went to Genesis and read when God said, "Let us make man in our image."

Gershon quickly said, "You Christians, that is not Trinity that you believe, it is the angels and God."

Jeff asked him to turn to Genesis 18 where Abraham had lunch with three visitors. We told him that one of the visitors was Adonai (The Lord) in a physical body having lunch with Abraham. He said it does not say Adonai but when he read it, he saw that it did say Adonai.

I said, "See, God became flesh and had lunch with Abraham."

He just scoffed at it. I then asked him to read Isaiah 53, all of it. After he read it I asked him who was the suffering servant. He quickly said that the suffering servant was Israel. Jeff asked him, "How could a people that needed a sacrifice be the sacrifice?" He got out from his desk chair and came and stood right in front of me. I didn't know what he was going to do.

He said, "Stand up, Brian, and give me a squeeze. You are a righteous man, you come to my house and my wife will cook for you."

Becoming the Executive Vice President for our ministry has been such a blessing. Being a missionary has been exciting. The only thing that Connie and I have had to get used to is that we must ask for financial support. However, God has provided for me to travel and has met our needs.

God has always provided. We have learned if we take care of God's business, He will provide for us. Jesus said that His yoke is light and for us to give Him ours. His yoke or burden is people being saved. I think it is a great trade off. Serve Him by sharing what He did for us by dying and being raised from the dead so that we may have eternal life. What a privilege to do that.

Line Drive

Coming to Georgia to be close to our son and daughter was no doubt what God wanted us to do. Being a close family is such a big thing. We came to help them. God provided what I was supposed to do. Little did I know that they were going to help me more than I helped them.

The Call: Mission Work

God has a purpose for each of us. Sometimes the purpose is different from what we think, but His purpose is always better than we can imagine. The last chapters reveal how my family is helping me more than I am helping them. This book is for them, especially my grandchildren. It is a book of hope and faith. It is a book that I pray has given you hope and faith. Life has twists and turns and can be difficult. God has brought Connie and me through difficult times and into our dreams.

CHAPTER 35

The Call: Parkinson's Disease

Traveling all around the globe was exciting, but I was not feeling well. My right arm and hand had become numb and shaking. I went to a spine specialist at Emory and had an MRI and CAT Scan. They found out the C6 and C7 were in bad shape. He told us that I needed surgery to fuse the vertebrae together. Five years earlier I had the C4 and C5 fused while I was in Ft. Lauderdale.

Before Dr. Rodts at Emory did the surgery, my health deteriorated to the point a brain MRI was ordered. Connie and I went to see a movement disorder specialist at Emory, Dr. Silver, to reveal the results of the MRI. He did some tests and confirmed that I had Parkinson's Disease. I quickly said that he was wrong; my shaking and numbness was due to the neck injury. He wrote out a prescription for a Parkinson's med and said he would not have written the prescription if he was not sure.

I left knowing that he was wrong. I had the surgery and got all feeling back in my arm and hand. It was back to normal except my hand and arm did not quit shaking. I told Connie I knew the shaking would quit once my rehab was over. However, rehab did not help the shaking, plus all my bones were really hurting. On a scale of 1 to 10, I was at 10. I couldn't sleep. I was getting maybe two hours of sleep a night.

Connie asked me to watch a video that Michael J. Fox had on You Tube. Early on a Sunday morning, I watched the video. When Connie got up, I told her that I had Parkinson's Disease. She went to a cabinet in the kitchen and pulled out some medication. She had filled the prescription for Parkinson's medication Dr. Silver had prescribed. I took the medicine and saw improvement in three days.

Half of this book has been written by Dragon, a device that allows me to speak and the computer prints my words. Connie is my personal ghostwriter. I have gone through leukemia and know I am going through a disease that is supposed to be progressive. Additionally, I am one in five hundred who has the disease that has acute bone pain, called Central Pain Syndrome.

> **Well, all I can say is nothing is going to steal my joy.**

So here is what God has done. I can't travel around the world like I did. God has me training missionaries here in my home. My son, Kirk, finds our interns host homes and trains them in baseball. Then, if the Lord directs them, they come to my house and I train them in evangelism, theology, cultural awareness, and how to raise support for their ministries. We train these men and women for six months before they go out into the field that is ripe for harvest. I am doing more ministry now than I have ever have. I am now the pastor to our missionaries.

> **My God is so good.**

Line Drive

Definitely our ways are not God's ways. His ways are always better than ours. Yes, I have Parkinson's Disease, but because I have Parkinson's Disease, Global Baseball has grown larger and will continue to grow. One of the reasons is that I cannot travel so I can see the trees and the forest at the same time. I now am the trainer of missionaries. I am now the pastor to our missionaries. I am having more fun now than I have ever had.

Being a competitor, I have started playing golf about once a week. My goal is to break 80. As I am writing this book, during the past 3 weeks, I have shot a 78, a 77, and a 76. God is so good.

I challenge you in whatever state you are in, never quit growing in Christ and never, ever let anything or anyone steal your joy. Depression can creep into your life. To break that depression, find a way to give yourself away. Find somebody that you can help and edify.

> *The joy of the Lord is my strength!*

Even if you are homebound, you have a phone and probably an email account. Also, you have multi-media. Get on Facebook and go through your friends and the Holy Spirit will stop you and have you pray for several people. One of the best ways to give yourself away is intercession.

CHAPTER 36

The Call: Brian Doyle Day?

The call came one afternoon. It was one of the owners of the Yankees AAA Minor League Team, Grant Cagle. He asked if it would be okay if they honored me and raised money for research of Parkinson's Disease. I was so surprised that I was speechless. Finally, I said it would be an honor to raise money for Parkinson's Disease research.

Grant had spoken to the New York Yankees and the event was to be held at the Yankee AAA PNC Field after the Yankee Old Timers Day, June 21, 2015. Grant also asked me if I would throw out the first pitch. Again, I said, "Yes."

How were the three owners of the Scranton/Wilkes Barre Yankees going to get enough Yankee Old Timers to go to Pennsylvania to raise money? God did it. I was constantly getting text messages from Grant telling me who was coming. Eventually, we had over thirty Yankee Old Timers present. The players were not called Yankee Old Timers during this game; they were called Legends.

2015 – Our Family at the Old Timers Day and Legends Game Weekend

2015 - Scranton/Wilkes-Barre, AAA Yankee team
"Legends Game, Brian Doyle Day"
Raised $40K for Parkinson's Research

The Call: Brian Doyle Day?

I had always desired to conduct a Chapel Service for my team when I was playing for the Yankees. I called Grant and said why don't we have a Chapel Service this Sunday and he said it was a great idea. I told him that I wanted to lead it. He said great and that he would pick the room for us to use.

When we got to the clubhouse they had tables with food ready to eat. I immediately thought this was going to hinder getting the guys to come to chapel, but discovered the only way to have chapel was to conduct it while they were eating.

> **Once again God allowed me to experience my dream of conducting chapel for my teammates. What a God I serve!**

So, I got in the middle of the clubhouse and said, "Hey guys, this is Sunday. We all can remember how we had chapel every Sunday. Well, I am going to give a chapel. I love it because everyone here wants to eat, and you do not have a choice but to hear what I have to say."

I started by talking about a nine-year-old boy sitting on a cardboard second base in a plowed-under corn field.

By the time I was done, I let them know that God had given me my dream and that He still gives me dreams. I told them, "Just seek God, delight in Him, and He will do it for you." There was not a dry eye in the room.

Line Drive

*Whether you are nine or ninety, if you are not dreaming you are not living. I really want you to think about that. I also want to remind you that the largest nation in the world is your imagi-**nation**. It took quite a long time to experience my dream of sharing the Gospel with my teammates in a chapel setting, but God is AWESOME!*

The New York Yankees Old Timer's Day: June 12, 2016

It was an amazing day; no, it was an epic day. The 2016 Yankee Old Timers' Day was held during the seventieth year of the Yankees having such a day. The fans love it. It is all about Yankee pride and tradition. The Yankees have won twenty-seven World Championships. Yankee fans are the most knowledgeable baseball fans in the world. They remember the history of the best-known brand in all the world—The New York Yankees.

The score was 3-3 with a man on third base and everyone in the dugout was shouting "let Doyle hit." I was coaxed into going to the plate. The last thing that an athlete wants to do is embarrass himself in front of 45,000 people. By the grace of God, I hit a hard, line drive to right field which was the "walk off hit" that ended the Old Timers' Game.

It was epic. All the guys came running out of the dugout to give me a hug. Half of these wonderful men had tears in their eyes. That will probably be my last at bat. How could one end it any better? Having Parkinson's Disease and batting in the winning run. That particular part of my life I FINISHED STRONG!

CHAPTER 37

The Call: From the Batter's Box to Home

A few years after I had become part of Global Baseball, the Lord gave me an opportunity to help design a special bat. This bat had a black handle. The bat had a white oval on the sweet part of the barrel. In this white oval there is a picture of Jesus on the cross. His blood is trickling down the handle. At the top of the bat in white letters are the verses that have been labeled, "The Roman Road." It has been given that name because each of the four verses come from the book of Romans in the New Testament. They also represent the steps one needs to take to become a child of God and a follower of Jesus Christ.

The Call: From the Batter's Box to Home

2013 - Global Baseball in Cuba, holding The Gospel Bat

To play the game of baseball, you need to leave the bench and step up to the plate. It is the same as life. Each of us must play the game of life. The main rule in the game of life is to know that there is a God. Allow me to share with you, Romans 1:20, "For since the creation of the world God's invisible qualities. . .his eternal power and divine nature. . .have been clearly seen, being understood from what has been made, so that people are without excuse."

You grab the bat and grip the black handle. That black handle represents that each of us has hold of our sin.

When you run to first base, you must let go of your sin (let go of the bat). First base represents Romans 3:23,

"For all have sinned and fall short of the glory of God." Once you understand that then you can go to second base.

Second base represents Romans 6:23, "For the penalty of sin is death." Now you are in scoring position because you know what sin is and what it can do to you. Now you can go to third base.

Third base represent Romans 5:8, "But God demonstrates his own love for us in this: While we were still sinners, Christ died for us."

> **If you want the promise, you need to do something for it.**

WOW! You are almost home. You now know you are a sinner. That the penalty of your sin is death. Yet God loves you so much that He sent Jesus to die for your sin. Now you have to score.

Home plate represents salvation. Romans 10:9-10 says, "If you declare with your mouth, 'Jesus is Lord,' and believe in your heart that God raised him from the dead, you will be saved. For it is with your heart that you believe and are justified, and it is with your mouth that you profess your faith and are saved."

If you've never done this before, it's easy. The Bible says in Romans 10:13, "Everyone who calls on the name of the Lord will be saved."

Line Drive

The first thing all of us need to do is to be sure that we're in His family. Those who aren't in the family of God need to repent from our sins. Second, we need to repent for trying to fix ourselves. Third, we need to pray that God will reveal our emptiness. Remember, God will only fill us to the point of our emptiness. Fourth, we all need to pray that He will fill us, and then fifth, believe that He will.

Our God is more than enough!

What is so cool, Connie and I did that at the very same time in different cities!

CHAPTER 38

The Call: Finish Strong

My desire is to finish strong and give myself away wherever I can. Jesus gave Himself away by dying on the cross. I want to be the person that Paul described and begged the Romans to become. He said, "I urge you brothers by the mercy of God to present yourselves as a **living sacrifice**, holy and acceptable to Him, which is your reasonable act of service (the least you can do)" (Romans 12:1 emphasis added).

Come with me on an adventurous journey. I am still just as adventurous as when Blake and I were in diapers. This adventure that I desire for you to be on with me is the ultimate in adventures. It is becoming a living sacrifice and making a difference in this world.

The Call: Finish Strong

You may think, how can I make a difference? I don't know, but God does. He took a little boy from just between Chicken Bristle, Uno, Cub Run, and Knob Lick and made a difference with him. I didn't know how He was going to do it, but He did. My life is full of joy because of Him.

> **Come with me and let each of us FINISH STRONG!**

I cannot teach anything that I haven't learned. I have learned being a follower of Jesus Christ has never disappointed me.

THE DESIRE TO FINISH STRONG

June 12, 2016: An Epic Day - Yankee Old Timers' Day

Having Parkinson's Disease and batting in the winning run. That part of my life I have FINISHED STRONG!

2016 - The uniform in honor of Yogi and the tip of the hat in honor of ALL the faithful NY Yankee fans

1966 - Denny's first professional team, The Spartanburg Phillies

1971 - .489 batting average and 35 RBI's. Not a bad year

1971 - Yes, Blake is ambidextrous, pitched LH and played 2B RH

1975 - Banquet honoring Denny - Dad, Mom, Janice, Blake, Denny, and Brian

1975 - Banquet honoring Denny with our wives Martha, Jean Anne, and Connie

2008 - Finally, Connie gets to step foot onto the field at Yankee Stadium

The Call

2018 - Connie and me on the shore of Cuba

2018 - Finishing Strong Together

Contact and Book Ordering Information
brianconniedoyle.globalsports@gmail.com